THE MANAGEMENT OF A MAJOR ULSTER ESTATE
IN THE LATE EIGHTEENTH CENTURY

T0165679

Maynooth Studies in Irish Local History

SERIES EDITOR Raymond Gillespie

This is one of six new pamphlets in the Maynooth Studies in Irish Local History Series to be published in the year 2001 which brings the number published to forty. Like their predecessors most of the pamphlets are based on theses completed as part of the M.A. in local history programme in National University of Ireland, Maynooth. While the regions and time span which they cover are diverse, from Cork city to Tyrone, they all share a conviction that the exploration of the local past can shed light on the evolution of modern societies. They each demonstrate that understanding the evolution of local societies is important. The local worlds of Ireland in the past are as complex and sophisticated as the national framework in which they are set. The communities which peopled those local worlds, whether they be the inhabitants of large cities, housing on the edge of those cities or rural estates, shaped and were shaped by their environments to create a series of inter-locking worlds of considerable complexity. Those past worlds are best interpreted not through local administrative divisions, such as the county, but in human units: local places where communities of people lived and died. Untangling what held these communities together, and what drove them apart, gives us new insights into the world we have lost.

These pamphlets each make a significant contribution to understanding Irish society in the past. Together with thirty-four earlier works in this series they explore something of the hopes and fears of those who lived in Irish local communities in the past. In doing so they provide examples of the practice of local history at its best and show the vibrant discipline which the study of local history in Ireland has become in recent years.

Maynooth Studies in Irish Local History: Number 35

The Management of a Major Ulster Estate in the Late Eighteenth Century

The Eighth Earl of Abercorn and his Irish Agents

William H. Crawford

IRISH ACADEMIC PRESS

DUBLIN • PORTLAND, OR

First published in 2001 by
IRISH ACADEMIC PRESS
44, Northumberland Road, Dublin 4, Ireland
and in the United States of America by
IRISH ACADEMIC PRESS
c/o ISBS, 5824 NE Hassalo Street, Portland, OR 97213–3644.

website: www.iap.ie

© William H. Crawford 2001

British Library Cataloguing in Publication Data
Crawford, W.H. (William Henry), 1932–
 The management of a major Ulster estate in the late eighteenth century: the
 eighth Earl of Abercorn and his Irish agents. – (Maynooth studies in Irish local
 history; no. 35)
 1. Hamilton, James   2. Landowners – Ireland – Biography
 I. Title
 941.5'07'092
 ISBN 0–7165–2743–x

A catalog record of this book is available from the Library of Congress

All rights reserved. Without limiting the rights under copyright reserved alone,
no part of this publication may be reproduced, stored in or introduced into a
retrieval system, or transmitted, in any form or by any means (electronic,
mechanical, photocopying, recording or otherwise), without the prior
written permission of both the copyright owner and the above
publisher of this book.

Typeset in 10 pt on 12 pt Bembo by
Carrigboy Typesetting Services, County Cork
Printed by Creative Print and Design (Wales) Ebbw Vale

Contents

Preface

O ver the years I have enjoyed my visits to Maynooth to meet the students of the M.A. course in local history and the welcoming atmosphere of the research institute at Drumcondra presided over by Bernadette Cunningham and Raymond Gillespie. I hope they will accept this publication as an appreciation for their kindness to me and for their efforts to stimulate local history studies in Ireland. Since I was first introduced to the great collection deposited in the Public Record Office of Northern Ireland by the duke of Abercorn, I have studied it with pleasure and quoted from it in a variety of publications. Even in this one I realise that I am still only scratching the surface and so my hope is that other historians will accept the challenge to exploit the riches of this collection. For my part, I wish to thank His Grace the duke of Abercorn and also the Deputy Keeper of the Records for permission to publish copious and extensive quotations from these letters.

Brian Trainor made available to us all the preliminary catalogue of the collection and transcribed very many extracts from the letters. Anthony Malcomson has completed that task and written an excellent introduction to the whole collection of the Abercorn estate papers, which may be downloaded from the PRONI website at *proni.nics.gov.uk*.

I am grateful to my old friend, Michael Cox, now resident in Scotland, for tracking source material about the activities in Scotland of the eighth earl of Abercorn. My thanks go also to William Roulston who has encouraged me by his own research in the Abercorn estate papers and, as a resident on one of the original Abercorn manors, corrected some of my errors of fact.

For giving me the opportunity to enjoy a career in historical research my debt is to my mother, who came from Castlederg in County Tyrone as Nina Robinson. My wife, Joan, has sustained that interest and made projects feasible. All my publications are dedicated to them.

Introduction

The loss of the archives of so many of the great Irish estates may preclude a thorough assessment of the contribution of the landlord class to Irish life but it should not prevent us from exploring those records that have survived in order to consider the nature of the authority its members exercised and how they used it. In 1812 Edward Wakefield in his survey *An account of Ireland, statistical and political* blamed Irish land agents for the backwardness of Irish estate management and suggested that their work consisted only of receiving the rents twice a year and setting out the turf-bogs in lots every spring.[1] In the absence of any defence these ill-considered charges soon assumed the status of a canon in Irish history. Correspondence, however, that has survived for a major estate in the north-west of Ireland, provides extensive and valuable evidence for the examination of the major factors affecting the administration of the estate while drawing attention to many other issues that are often overlooked or misunderstood. It is especially valuable that this landlord had been reared in Scotland while his agents were all Irishmen raised and schooled in the very different Irish version of English law: very often they had to spell out legal niceties that might require to be interpreted in reaching decisions. Although generalisation about the landlord system in Ireland cannot be made from the affairs of a single estate, the issues raised here may encourage others to study estate correspondence with more confidence and use it effectively in studying other aspects of Irish history.

This great collection, known as the Abercorn correspondence, has been transferred from Baronscourt, the Irish seat of the duke of Abercorn, to the Public Record Office of Northern Ireland in Belfast where it is available for consultation as a section of the Abercorn estate collection under its catalogue reference D/623.[2] It was surveyed by the archivists from Belfast in the 1950s and early 1960s and one of them, Brian Trainor, was so impressed by the quality of the letters that he was cataloguing, that he spent many hours of his free time transcribing them. It was from these transcripts that Canon John Gebbie, rector of the parish of Ardstraw, made his own selection of extracts for *An introduction to the Abercorn letters* which he published in 1972.[3] The political correspondence relating to the borough of Strabane in County Tyrone was then exploited by Anthony Malcomson.[4] The collection has more recently been used to a considerable extent by Martin Dowling and later by John Dooher in several chapters contributed to *The fair river valley: Strabane through the ages.*[5]

Such a great collection will always attract historians and it does deserve a detailed study of the quality of W. A. Maguire's *The Downshire estates in Ireland 1801–1845*[6] as well as a host of local studies focussing on the development of the economy and society of individual manors and districts. This publication has the more limited purpose of encouraging students and historians to tackle estate correspondence. To transmit the range, quality, and tone of the correspondence, it is imperative to use extensive quotations to explain the issues and transactions under review and identify the changes that took place on the Abercorn estate in the late eighteenth century. Unfortunately, it has proved necessary also to omit several themes that could be described as peripheral to these main issues.

The subject may be broken down into three main themes: the character of the landlord and his agents, relations between landlord and tenants, and the economic and social development of the estate. First we need to examine the character and aims of the eighth earl of Abercorn as the absentee owner of these extensive estates. Did he have an explicit overall strategy for the estate and how did he intend to apply it ? Was it responsive or proactive? How were his agents selected? Of what character were they? How closely were they supervised? What were their basic duties? How were they required to act in society? What role did seneschals and their manor courts play in sorting out everyday problems on the estate? What auxiliary skills, such as surveying and map-making, did the landlord encourage to improve the administration of the estate?

The second theme of relations between landlord and tenants raises many issues especially because it is difficult to determine which party held the initiative in this ongoing contest. Although the terms of the contract between the parties were set out in the lease with several clauses and covenants (promises to carry out certain undertakings such as hedging and ditching), they had become almost impossible to enforce at law by the mid-eighteenth century. Negotiations for a lease concentrated on its length in terms of years or lives or both, and on the new rent. Little was said about the problems that might arise. The most serious was non-payment of rent for which the landlord's remedy was first *distress* (seizing goods to the value of the debt) and then *reentry* (to re-assume ownership of the property). In fact *ejectment* (getting rid of an unsatisfactory tenant) had become a lengthy and extensive legal process. Of increasing importance was the concept of *tenant right* because its ramifications penetrated everywhere and exacerbated relations between landlord and tenant. The use of sale and entry *fines* by Abercorn to control changes in its tenantry introduces a fresh theme. Vital topics in the rural history of Ulster have been the processes of *subletting* and *subdivision*. Perhaps one of the most surprising revelations in the correspondence is the extent to which the agents were expected to settle disputes between tenants. Two cases, those of John McNeelans of Shanoney and Edward French, have been reconstructed from the correspondence to illustrate how difficult and even intransigent tenants could be to each other.

The third section examines the role that the estate played in providing essential services for the tenants, promoting projects for the community at large, encouraging tenants to improve their holdings, and exploiting the potential of the estate. Among the services for the tenants were the promotion and supervision of markets and fairs, the maintenance of corn mills, the organisation of turbary and the recovery of bog timber, the construction of kilns for producing lime, the protection of fisheries, and the supervision of ferries across the broad river Foyle. There was also at least an implicit policy that supported and encouraged all tenants to reclaim marginal land, enclose fields with either hedges or stone walls, and adopt improved methods of farming. In parallel with this the estate pursued an active policy of searching for minerals, especially coal and lead, and cultivating and preserving timber. Even more important for the future prosperity of the estate was the active role played by its management in promoting communications projects such as the construction of a canal linking Strabane to the river Foyle and the development of an extensive network of roads.

By concentrating on the rural aspects of the estate, this essay excludes several important topics that are well covered in the correspondence. By far the most substantial is the development of the borough of Strabane, especially during and after the struggle for control over the corporation. The authorities had to find money to administer the growing town and to organise schemes to cope with food shortages and natural disasters such as flooding, on three occasions in the 1770s. Other important topics that have had to be omitted are the payment of tithes, the antiquated formulae for levying the county cess, the campaign to suppress illicit distillation, and the maintenance of law and order.

In 1761 Edward Willes, then chief baron of the Irish court of Exchequer, was impressed with the spirit of improvement then permeating Ireland and in his dealings with the grand juries throughout the country, he could perceive 'that a man makes a figure in his country in proportion to the improvements he makes. You hear him complimented on his having encouraged any branch of manufacture, or draining and reclaiming so much bog or mountain, sowing so much flax, tilling so many acres of wheat, planting so many trees, etc.'[7] His comments accord well with the substance of this publication but they give only a brief concept of the activities and initiatives that were channeled through the estate office.

Landlord and Agents

A mong the most extensive estates in Ulster were those belonging to the Abercorn family in the basin of the River Foyle in north-west Ulster. The whole estate comprises much of the district lying within a ten mile radius of the town of Strabane, some fourteen miles south of and upstream from the city of Derry. Under the Ulster Plantation scheme, James Hamilton, the first earl of Abercorn, with two of his brothers and a brother-in-law, all Scots, were each granted substantial proportions in the barony of Strabane in the north-western corner of County Tyrone. Although several of the manors belonging to their descendants were confiscated by the Cromwellians in the 1650s and by the Crown in the 1690s, they were all regained finally by the sixth earl in 1703.[1] By 1790 the annual rental of the estate was almost £20,000. It comprised almost 60,000 acres in the four Tyrone manors of Cloghogle, Derrygoon, Donelong and Strabane and the Donegal manor of Mongavlin (fig. 1), all names that appear regularly in the correspondence between the eighth earl and his Irish agents.

In 1744 James Hamilton (born 1712) succeeded his father, the seventh earl (1734–44), to become the eighth earl of Abercorn. His main English residence was at Witham in Essex where he was to entertain Queen Charlotte on her arrival in Britain in 1761. In 1745 he purchased from the duke of Argyll the barony of Duddingston, close to Holyrood House on the outskirts of Edinburgh: there Sir William Chambers built one of the finest classical houses in Britain for him in the years between 1763 and 1768. Chambers also built him a town house in Grosvenor Square in London in 1763. In 1764 Abercorn also reacquired the former Scottish property of the family, known as the lordship of Paisley in Renfrewshire, and laid out a suburb, or 'new town', around the abbey in the 1770s. He died in 1789, unmarried, and was buried in Paisley Abbey where his memorial hangs on the north wall.[2] It was said of him that 'he never drank anything but water, nor had he more relish for the society of women'.[3]

Abercorn visited his Irish estates and resided in the family seat at Baronscourt in west Tyrone on only a few occasions: in 1746, 1749, 1751, 1752, 1756, 1761, 1777 (April to December 'after an absence of fifteen years'), and 1782. He was an absentee landlord by all the definitions of that term and yet the scale, the range and the substance of the correspondence he maintained with his Irish agents, reveals the extent and depth of his knowledge of life on the estates. Several of his agents kept him well-informed and in the years between 1757

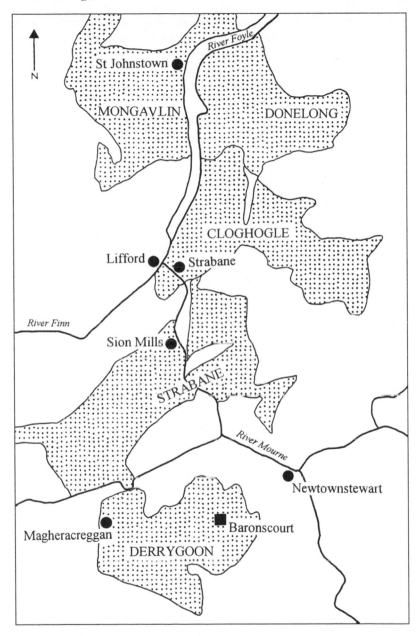

1. The Abercorn Estates in Ulster

and the earl's death in 1789, one of them, also named James Hamilton, wrote very detailed letters that enabled the earl to make decisions on a wide variety of matters. Because the earl's correspondence has survived also, it is possible to gain some understanding about material and social conditions on the Abercorn estate in the late eighteenth century and to analyse many of the issues that were important to those who lived at that time.

Although Abercorn must have had plenty of problems to cope with on his side of the Irish Sea, his letters to his Irish agents reveal that he was guided by a clear set of principles. He has been referred to by Anthony Malcomson in his study of the family as 'the consolidator' of the Abercorn estates and he was particularly vigilant in securing his rents, protecting his rights and interests, and maintaining his authority. He listened to the advice of his agents, encouraged them to be active throughout the estate, and supported them in public. At the same time he persevered with his plans to develop the resources and infrastructure of the estate. He was shrewd in devising and applying strategies that maintained a wholesome discipline on the estate. Since he was well aware that Scottish law differed fundamentally from English (and hence from Irish) law, he tried to obtain the best legal advice about the courses of action open to him. At the same time he was prepared always to champion his tenants against legal threats from neighbouring landowners, especially over boundary disputes, and from the clergy of the Established Church, although he did support the clergy on the estates. He took seriously his duty to look after the welfare of his tenants through the system of estate management and to provide them with access to local justice through his manor courts. His correspondence reveals how much time and energy was expended by his agents and himself in preventing and settling disputes between tenants. By the time of his death in 1789 the estate had acquired an excellent reputation.

Perhaps the best clues to Abercorn's character are to be found in his letter of 1 August 1753, replying to one from the rector of the parish of Ardstraw, the Rev. Dr Pelissier:

> This day I was favoured with your letter, and shall very readily employ my influence to establish a good agreement between you and the parishioners. If you write to me in consequence of any difference that has arisen, I am truly quite a stranger to it. And if your apprehension of combinations against you is only general, it is, I hope, without foundation because I do not recollect to have heard of anything of that nature in the parish. But as you are much unacquainted with it, give me leave to hint to you, to be cautious of believing complaints and suggestions that may be made to you, until you have examined them. In such a number of people, you must expect to find some that will be wrong-headed and absurd. But you will see that kind usage will operate

strongly upon the majority, and the more because they are little accustomed to it; I do not mean in tithe matters only.

Whenever I have said anything to my tenants about their tithes, my advice has been such as I think best calculated to preserve peace and quiet, and extremely simple. It is this: to agree for their tithes, when they can do it to advantage; when they can not, to set them out in the fairest manner.

My way of thinking upon this matter, is so perfectly well known to my agents, that nothing I can say to them will explain it. But if you think it necessary to show them this letter, they will look upon it as a mark of my inclination to contribute to your ease, and will endeavour to do the same themselves.[4]

There is no hint of condescension in this letter which Abercorn injected with just the right amount of gravity. He set out not only to calm and reassure the agitated cleric that there was no conspiracy against him but also to encourage him to treat his parishioners with kindness and consideration, even if some of them were bound to behave in a wrong-headed and absurd manner. The whole tone of the letter was designed to lower the temperature and encourage the recipient to reflect again about his problems. The final paragraph is masterly: Abercorn was showing his confidence in the quality of the men he had chosen to look after his people and their welfare.

Anthony Malcomson confirms this view of the earl's character in his study of the strategy and tactics used by Abercorn to win back political control over the borough of Strabane in 1764:

Abercorn had shown that he wanted merely to be restored to what he considered to be his own and not to revenge himself on his dispossessors. In this he displayed a restraint remarkable among borough patrons in an age when boroughs were regarded as a species of private property and opposition to the patron as an invasion of property rights.[5]

The agents through whom Abercorn administered the Irish estate were local men well acquainted with local attitudes and customs. When he took control of the estate in 1744, he had to deal with three agents: John McClintock of Dunmore, Jo. Colhoun of Corncamon [or Coarncampble], and Nathaniel Nisbitt of Lifford, all resident in County Donegal. When Nisbitt was confirmed in his office in 1744, he thanked Abercorn with the words: 'As my uncle was an old servant in your Lordship's family, and I hope I have behaved myself always with the character of an honest man, we humbly beg your Lordship may confer the honour on us of my still continuing your Lordship's servant.'[6] Nisbitt was to claim later in 1757 that he had served the family for twenty-six years.[7] All three of the agents were continued by the new earl. At least two of them, Nisbitt and McClintock, held other agencies from substantial landowners, as the third agent reminded the earl on a suitable occasion:

> If your Lordship pleases to consider Mr McClintock's agency from your Lordship and that he is agent to all Mr McCausland's rents and some others besides and a good fortune of his own, and Mr Nathaniel Nisbitt has two good agencies, Mr Creighton's and Mr Montgomery's, and a good fortune of his own and no charge as to children, I shall be greatly thankful and well satisfied with whatever your Lordship does, though I have the least business and smallest fortune and family of children.[8]

All of them, however, had profited from their job in various ways suggested by Nathaniel Nisbitt after he became the sole surviving agent. He explained to the earl in 1757 how he himself operated the Irish system of remuneration to agents:

> The common allowance for agents in this country is 12*d*. in the £ [5 per cent]; whatever less is given is given by agreement, according as the circumstances of things may be; I have several times computed what I had for your Lordship's money, and I never could make it 9*d*. in the £, the fees or nominy peny[9] inclusive, paid by the tenants, for I never trusted them so, as to let it swell; Mr McClintock and Mr Colhoun made more than I did, and McClintock more than Colhoun again; your Lordship might have heard they trusted the tenants longer than I did, and when I saw real distress I never charged anything, and your Lordship knows they had little bargains of land which I never had, and other little dealings among the people which I thought below me, choosing always to keep within the law, well knowing that the Lord Chancellor's allowance was 12*d*. in the £ on a sequestered estate; indeed in most estates in this country the 12*d*. in the £ is paid by the tenants by covenant as receiver's fees if the rent was paid in 21 days after due; remember your Lordship bid me speak freely, which I am determined to do and hide nothing from your Lordship.[10]

After two of the agents died in service, John McClintock in 1751 and Jo. Colhoun in 1755, Nathaniel Nisbitt agreed to take on the management of the whole estate[11] but within two years he was suffering from the strain and advised the earl to appoint an agent for each of the five manors.[12] In a subsequent letter he recommended two brothers, 'fat Jack' (John who died in January 1788) and Jemmy (James) Hamilton, and Mr John Sinclair, 'a rough honest man', whose family held the freehold of Hollyhill from Abercorn. At the close of 1757 Nisbitt provided Abercorn with the rentals of the Tyrone manors:

whole manor of Strabane (and new purchase) . . . . . . £2,381. 10s. 4d.
Donelong manor . . . . Mr John Sinclair, agent . . . . . £1,932. 10s. 8d.
Cloghogle manor . . . . Mr John Hamilton, agent . . . £1,176. 6s. 0d.
Derrygoon manor . . . Mr James Hamilton agent . . . £1,271. 10s. 0d.[13]

Although Jemmy Hamilton had been given the manor with the fewest tenants, Nisbitt assured Abercorn that he would be kept busy managing Abercorn's mansion at Baronscourt and its demesne. Indeed, Jemmy's correspondence about Baronscourt gives the impression that it underwent a continuous process of maintenance and refurbishment. Nisbitt himself retained the manor of Strabane as well as the Donegal manor until he was dismissed in January 1764 after a mental collapse: his nephew, who sorted out his affairs, informed the earl that he was expecting to inherit a fortune of eight thousand pounds.[14]

The pulse of the estate could best be monitored in the towns on market and fair days when the agent met every rank of tenant and cottier and was appraised of the current problems of the local economy, its commerce, professions, trades, and industries. Nathaniel Nisbitt emphasized the importance of the presence of the landlord or his agent in the markets and fairs when he assured Abercorn: 'I was not a market day absent from Strabane since a long time before your Lordship was in this country, nor one absent from St Johnstown since your Lordship ordered markets to be held there, . . . '.[15]

The major roles of every agent were to secure for the landlord the rents due from the tenants every half year and to protect his rights. In the furtherance of this duty the agent acted as his representative in negotiating new leases with the tenants. He also played a vital role in the welfare of the community. In managing all these affairs he had at all times to retain the confidence of the earl, a task made more difficult by tenants who went to lay their cases before the landlord at the residence he happened to be occupying in either England or Scotland.

The chief agent was required to play a major role not only in looking after the welfare of the tenants but also in promoting the economic and social development of the estate. Far from being given a free hand to administer the estate as he saw fit, however, he was required to provide a strategic view of the whole estate, assess priorities and explain the issues involved in sufficient detail for the earl to make a decision. In all this he had to remember that as the earl had been raised in Scotland under a very different legal jurisdiction, he was therefore unlikely to be aware of many laws, customs, and traditions that would have been familiar to an Irish landowner. He was required to notify him about any problems that required him to take a decision or affected any of his rights: such decisions might require good judgment and experience. He was expected to provide leadership in times of crisis in the community, such as the food shortages of 1745 and 1770–1 and the serious flooding of the town on several occasions in the 1770s, or when tenants threatened to get out of control, as in the heyday of the Volunteers. He had to be prepared to sort out problems and resolve quarrels, although as Jemmy Hamilton once confessed to the earl, this might be done by proxy:

> As there are sometimes trivial disputes between them, to save them trouble I name two to settle them, and he in general [John Kinkead] one of them, if it is near him, as I thought him honest and knowing in such matters; by this he gets the odium of one of the parties who, where they are interested, seldom judge impartially, and therefore suspect him of partiality. I have acted thus not to save myself any little trouble, but them, as I think myself in the strongest manner bound by duty and gratitude to act in everything for your Lordship's interest and that of your Lordship's people and will always have pleasure in doing so . . . [16]

Abercorn appreciated the advice of his agents, especially when they corresponded regularly and explained matters clearly and in sufficient detail. He did not always agree with the advice and certainly did not always accept it. As long as they treated him with the respect due to him, he encouraged them to broach difficult problems and to give their opinions on policy matters.

The tenants expected an agent to provide leadership especially in times of crisis and danger, and legal knowledge and wisdom in resolving quarrels between neighbours and members of families. They held him responsible for the proper behaviour of the officials under his authority, such as the bailiffs and the seneschal presiding over the manor courts. Many individuals throughout the estate relied on the active support of the agent: millers needed him to secure their customers and keep their mills in repair; builders wanted him to provide timber; farmers wanted him to construct limekilns; fishermen and ferrymen looked to him to protect their rights. Everyone expected him to exploit the potential of the estate: searching for minerals, especially coal and lead; and cultivating and preserving timber

If the estate were to prosper, the landlord needed to play a positive role in the county community. As Abercorn was resident mainly in Scotland or in England he had to rely on his friends, relations, and officials in Ulster to speak for him and he himself had to correspond with influential individuals on important matters. There were important developments and projects that required the earl to lobby other landowners or to negotiate with them directly.

MANOR COURTS

It was in response to all these matters that Abercorn decided to tighten up the administration of the manor courts on the estate. He had been informed in 1759:

> Mr Cary that holds the courts in Ballymagorry is gone to live in Derry which is a great loss to your Lordship's tenants as he does not hold any courts but at May and November; the reason is that if a man be in due but 5 shillings he must go to Omagh and have 9s. 6d. of cost which if decided in your Lordship's court there would be but 1s. 8d. of cost and time to make it up too and another greater hardship follows that the times they must go to Omagh is either in seed time or in harvest which is the two times we have our assizes.[17]

The matter cannot have been pressing because there were no further complaints to the earl until December 1765 when it was raised in similar terms by John Hamilton, the agent for Strabane manor. This time Abercorn replied by return of post: 'I desire you will think of a proper person for seneschal of the manors in the county of Tyrone, and inform me of him. I must have one that will hold the courts regularly every three weeks. At the same time acquaint Mr Cary that I find it necessary to appoint a person who is more conveniently situated to those manors.'[18] After consultation the three agents recommended Alexander McKernan who had served the estate well for seven years. They recommended too that the courts 'should be held monthly, that is the first Monday in the month for Donelong, Wednesday for Derrygoon, Friday for Cloghogle, and Saturday for Strabane ... The seneschal living in this town will be of great use to the different manors, as they have frequent business to it'.[19] Abercorn approved the appointment and the decision to hold the courts monthly, adding: 'I insist upon its being done regularly, even though there is no business ... '.[20]

After the death on 24 December 1779 of Daniel McKernan (who had succeeded Alexander McKernan as seneschal), several men applied to be considered for the post of seneschal. Among them was James Jordan, the then overseer of the bogs, who reminded the earl that he had petitioned him for the post at the death of Alexander McKernan and made this case for consideration:

> As my time is entirely spent about your Lordship's business and among the tenants, the addition of my being appointed seneschal for the whole, two, or any one of the manors, would not in the least interrupt my present business, but very much assist me to complete it, as many

disputes concerning trespass etc. ought to be prevented at the courts leet etc., a knowledge of which I have endeavoured to acquire, having been sworn an attorney in your Lordship's courts thirteen years ago, and since have read some of the best authors relative to the origin and practice of courts leet and courts baron'.[21]

Another candidate was Conn O'Donnell, Mr Hamilton's assistant, who reminded the earl that 'my grandfather Conn O'Donnell had the honour of being particularly known to your lordship, and as I am told, filled or wrote the first leases that were ever granted by your Lordship, and both he and my father Hugh O'Donnell were each in his lifetime tenants to your Lordship.' He claimed: 'I have often assisted the last seneschal in his duty, when his want of health rendered him incapable, and at times when the Recorder of this town was abroad, I have attended the Provost's court in his stead.'[22]

Both these applications remind us that the post of seneschal, like the post of agent on an estate, did not require professional qualifications but rather a period of apprenticeship to a practising lawyer. Men relied on the reputation of their families, their kinsfolk, and their connections to obtain an entry to this privileged world.

Landlord and Tenants

In the late eighteenth century the most characteristic element of Ulster life was still the landed estate that had been introduced in the early years of the seventeenth century. The right of the eighth earl of Abercorn to own and develop this estate had been granted by the crown under the scheme for the plantation of Ulster. Therefore, although this branch of the Hamilton family, the earls of Abercorn, were Scots, they were to hold their property in Ireland under English law. Although the crown permitted them to retain a proportion of the estate as demesne, it insisted that the remainder had to be leased to tenants according to forms of leases then current in England. This extension to Ireland of the English common-law system of property rights revolutionised landholding for it converted land into a marketable commodity, standardised land-measures and land-holding arrangements, and promoted the concept of private property. The crown had replaced traditional arrangements for holding land between lords and their men by insisting on the legally-binding contract of the lease which defined the rights and responsibilities of both landlord and tenant. In Ulster it had even resurrected an archaic concept by creating these new estates into manors in order to make the new landlords responsible for the welfare and discipline of their tenants through the manor courts.[1] Within a century of their creation these estates had begun to provide a very stable element in Ulster society. Even if individual owners failed, their estates could be purchased and developed by fresh landlords for there was a thriving market in property. The estates became notable for their continuity and the records that have survived, not only in the national archive institutions but also in the Registry of Deeds in Dublin, demonstrate their importance in Ulster, and indeed in Irish, society.

The major problem for any landlord in dealing with tenants on his estate, was to maintain his authority and the control of his property against the aspirations and greed of his tenants. Every tenant wanted a very long lease of as much land as he could possibly hold, guaranteed by the landlord in any court of law, preferably a fee farm grant or perpetuity, at a very low or nominal rent with no duties in kind or services to the landlord, and untrammelled by covenants that might restrict his right to use or abuse the property and the subtenants in any way he chose. In such a relationship, maintained in a perpetual state of tension, the laws made in parliament and the judgements made by the high courts were all important.

Throughout the seventeenth century the Abercorns, like other Ulster landowners, had tended to restrict leases to substantial tenants. In the eighteenth century they found that this became much less feasible. In 1749, for example, Nisbitt raised a common complaint among tenants everywhere:

> I have found the tenants complain of the short tenure they had, and seemed always to hold 21 year leases in great contempt, which they said hindered the improving their farms; some I believe it did hinder, and others I thought naturally slothful; if it was agreeable to your Lordship to give them lives instead of years, I do believe they would agree to pay as much rent as possibly they could; the country people is certainly very fond of this kind of tenure, and many landlords have indulged them in it though I think 21 years or three lives does not make a very great difference, yet some give 31 years after the expiration of three lives, which makes a great deal of difference.[2]

Abercorn never paid too much attention to such advice. The maximum term of leases on the rural part of the estate was limited to twenty-one years, probably by a family settlement, whereas many estates in Ulster granted three-life leases, that is leases that ran until the death of all three individuals named in the lease. Many of these leases in effect ran for more than fifty years. In Scotland the maximum period for a lease was nineteen years and many tenants had shorter terms. The earl was convinced from experience that the length of Ulster leases provided him with few opportunities to discipline his tenants and prod them to pay their rents more regularly and to improve their farms. His efforts to tighten up the leases drew warnings from his agents about the consequences some of his proposals might have on the Irish tenants. In 1757 Nisbitt, when broaching with Abercorn his own intention to give up his agency, felt in a strong enough position to expostulate:

> The clause [in the proposed new leases] against the tenants bequeathing or leaving to their families their interest in the [term of] twenty-one years, will I am afraid frighten them, and make them think that they have no interest in anything. Nay there are people in this country that would not value to tell them they were in a state of vassalage by it. They all now that are able [are] determined to improve but if this clause should meet with an ill-construction, it's my single opinion, for I consult nobody, it would do a great deal of hurt ... I would not have your Lordship give out any leases to such as have not paid off their old rents, for a new lease is a receipt for all former arrears ...[3]

Nisbitt knew that the prevailing culture on the estate would not have allowed Abercorn to enforce a clause depriving tenants of their customary rights to bequeath their interest to their families. It is unlikely, too, that the Irish judiciary would have supported such a drastic move at that time. Nisbitt's final comment may have been a timely reminder to Abercorn that legal practice in Ulster differed greatly from that in Scotland.

Nevertheless Abercorn became so exasperated by the failure of his Irish tenants to carry out the covenants in their leases that he decided to reduce the term of future leases to seven years: 'That term seems a very long one for a landlord to enter into covenants for, which he is expected to observe, with tenants who think themselves not bound on their part. I have suffered greatly by letting long leases and see the imprudence of it.'[4] Jemmy Hamilton, Abercorn's agent, replied a fortnight later:

> I will take the liberty of deferring till I may hear from your Lordship, letting the tenants know in the humour they are in, of going to America, that their new leases are to be but for seven years, knowing this might prevent some from purchasing, and some who are not able to hold might be continued; beside I fear it might make some of the good tenants endeavour to sell at whatever terms they could, not that I would incline by concealing it to deceive the purchaser, but in hopes that your Lordship might find reason to give them better tenures.[5]

The strength of Abercorn's feelings about this issue is clear from the language and tone of his next letter to Jemmy:

> I think it an act of lunacy to enter into covenants for a long term which I am bound and intend to perform, with people who profess not to think themselves bound on their parts. The only justification of letting leases even for seven years is that the shortness of the term may make the tenants reflect they cannot break their covenants with impunity ...[6]

Abercorn's resolution did not weaken. More than eight months later he reiterated his feelings in another letter to Jemmy's brother, John, the agent in Strabane: 'The great consolation I have in the oppression I lie under from the tenants is the resolution I have taken not to let farms any more for such long terms. Long leases are the ruin of Ireland and of every man in it and the great obstruction to improvement ... '.[7]

RENEWAL OF LEASES

In mid-eighteenth century Ulster it was still not difficult to obtain renewal of a lease if a tenant was in good standing on the estate. The lease was the common currency that men struggled to obtain and once secured, they were loathe to surrender. The eighteenth century saw tenants increase pressure on landlords by pressing claims for their *tenant right*, which they interpreted as the right to negotiate exclusively with their landlord the terms for the renewal of their lease.

This concept of tenant right appears to be grounded in the context of the Ulster Plantation settlement when colonists were bound to their new lords by something resembling the feudal tenure they had known before they left England. The Tenures Abolition Act (Ireland) Act of 1662 (14 & 15 Car. II c. 19), however, converted such feudal tenures into 'freeholds' and leaseholds based on written contracts, although some of the old paraphernalia such as 'suit to court and mills' and heriots were not abolished. Although tenants were no longer, in any sense, bound to their lords, many of them appreciated the traditional relationship and valued support and patronage in the colonial world. Those instincts were expressed in their claim to remain under their landlord and to hold their property from him, which is the essence of the concept of tenant right. On their behaviour as good and loyal tenants they based their claims to renewal of their tenancy.

The concept of tenant-right was invoked most often by those tenants whose performance during the term of the lease had not been up to standard. The lease required the tenant to pay his rent regularly and perform the covenants. Many tenants had to be badgered to pay their rents, even in good times, while covenants were more honoured in the breach than the observance. In 1757 when Jemmy Hamilton had taken over the manor of Derrygoon, he had treated leniently those tenants who had provided a variety of excuses for failing to pay their rents. By the time he succeeded Nisbitt in 1763 he had been hardened. Soon he, in turn, was apologising to the earl:

> It must be allowed even by the tenants themselves, that their bargains under your Lordship are good, which is very evident by the high prices given by anyone purchasing into your Lordship's estate, and I am persuaded that few amongst them, but could pay much better, and that it is now high time to oblige them, their leases having run so far. The richest among them plead for time to enable them to carry on trade, others that if they are obliged to pay they will be forced to sell their stock, or that they have their yarn ready to weave and that if they got some time they would make considerably by it . . . .[8]

Abercorn's initial response was to instruct Jemmy to inform all tenants who were in arrears that their claim to tenant-right would not be recognised when their leases expired. He decided, too, that more immediate pressure should be applied to the greatest offenders and took advice about evicting or ejecting those who were most heavily in arrears. In October 1769 the sheriff carried out the first eviction on the estate and Abercorn instructed his agent:

Ejecting tenants is so new a branch of business to me, that it is necessary to give some directions about the Cuninghams. Their readmission is totally out of the question. Be pleased to appoint two men to value the houses, and if they value them reasonably and fairly, add a fifth part to the valuation (that is four to every twenty) and let that sum be assigned to be paid to you at and before the entry of the new tenants. And set the lands by cant [auction], for the best rent that can be got, subject to the payment of that fine, and to the cottiers' bargain with the Cuninghams. And to prevent any collusion, make the rent, that the lands are to be set up at, not less than a fourth part more than the old rent. If there are no bidders, I will hold them in my own hands. Allow the fine, after payment of the costs, to go in discharge of part of the arrears, and recover the rest as soon as you can.[9]

The whole impetus was taken out of Abercorn's campaign, however, when he learned that Irish law granted anyone dispossessed on an ejectment the right to repossess his property if he paid the debt and costs within six months.[10] The legal process of ejectments was fraught with technicalities, as Jemmy had to report in May 1771: 'I had the ejectments served for the Manors of Strabane and Derrygoon, and of the eight but one of them is proper; in some of them all the livers on the lease were not served, in some the wrong term for the appearance.'[11] He was learning from experience. Because the tenants expected him to treat them fairly and with understanding, he had to devise strategies that they would find acceptable. The lease contract gave the landlord or his agent the right to seize, or *distrain* (the official term) property belonging to the tenant in lieu of the debt: this action was known as *distress*. After a certain period allowed to the tenant for paying off the debt (known as *recovery*, or *replevin*), the property could be sold in public to pay the debt. If the property seized was not sufficient to pay the arrears, the landlord had the right to *re-enter* and resume his property but only after every opportunity to repay the debt had been afforded to the tenant. When rents were long overdue, therefore, the agent sent out the estate bailiff to seize cattle. As Jemmy explained to the earl:

As soon as the cattle can be driven, I will endeavour to have the arrears cleared off, and think it would be best to drive the ablest for their November rents, as they can pay it with less hardship than many can their arrears, nor will my speaking, writing, or sending the bailiff to them be minded; they tell me there are others that owe more than they, that your Lordship would never bear harder on one than another. I do believe driving the rich which is by much the greatest part of them, would hurry those that are poorer, almost as effectually as if they were driven themselves.[12]

Throughout the years that they worked together, Jemmy was always aware of the fine line that he was expected to tread in dealing with the tenants. In August 1780 he could remind the earl: 'Your Lordship has in every instance that I have laid before you of an arrear being desperate, uniformly desired that I should forgo it rather than resort to expedients for recovering that might probably end in greater loss'.[13] Nevertheless, Jemmy was never sanguine about his chances of getting in the rents:

> If I could once get a farm sold cleverly I am very confident that some would struggle to pay, who as your Lordship observes, are awaiting the event, but the loss I am at is getting purchasers while the tenant is in possession. If he himself is not earnest in selling, not a man will offer to buy, and to bring the tenant to consent, I must either take off all he has, or bring a writ for him and send him to gaol. I will indeed do everything in my power. I will go on and seize the crops and cattle and if I can get sufficient security for their being delivered to me on the grounds in eight days, I will set up notices to sell them and the farm at that time. If I cannot get security I must, I believe, impound the cattle and sell them in six days after they are impounded, and then if there will not be sufficient, sell the farm if I can . . . [14]

Here Jemmy is pointing to the crux of the problem: how to get a purchaser while the tenant was still in possession. If he could solve that problem, he could satisfy the earl. He realised that the earl was not aware of the complexities of distress and re-entry and so he tried again in a letter a few days later:

> [Carlan] contents now to sell it but when it comes to the push may show an unwillingness [in order] to discourage a person who is ready otherwise to give what he thinks is a full value. I have found almost in all my trials that I could not have the business well completed and I am so baffled by them that sometimes I think of bringing writs, sometimes of ejecting, and sometimes of having them purchased in trust, and endeavouring to sell them afterwards – for if I sent some of them to gaol, there he would remain and I could do nothing with the farm. If I ejected, the expence and delay is great, and if a farm fell, as it were, in[to] my hand, they would endeavour to make it turn out to as little account as they could. Yet I will not be discouraged though perhaps there will be loss in some cases.[15]

On the following 22 April, however, he was expecting a reprimand when he wrote: 'I am really very vexed that the arrears has lessened little in the course of a year, and at a time when it cannot be denied, but that the seasons and markets were both favourable to the tenants'.[16] It arrived within the week and reminded him of his primary obligation to his employer. He could only respond:

> I received the honour of your Lordship's letter of the 16th and will very carefully and very seriously attend to the contents of it. I find I have been considering too much of expedients by which the tenants might get over their difficulties; had they been as attentive themselves as I wished to have been for them, they would have been before this pretty clear of debts that sucked their very vitals, and their rents much forwarder, but now I am determined to exert every power, and not to slack, till things are put on such a footing as your Lordship may direct; . . . [17]

Jemmy's strongest weapon in dealing with slow payers was to repeat that the earl would refuse to recognise a claim of tenant right from any tenant who did not pay one half year's rent before the next was due. This threat was likely to have more effect, if the tenants believed the earl was serious, because every tenant was concerned about obtaining the renewal of his lease. If the tenant could claim title to all the land in the holding when the term of his lease ran out, he was considered by his fellow-tenants to have tenant right and would have no competition from any of them when negotiating a new lease with his landlord. This need for the tenant to have full possession of all the land on his farm created a major problem on the estate because it conflicted with the tenant practice of subletting.

TENANTS SELLING FARMS

Abercorn maintained his control over his estate by insisting and ensuring by law that no tenant could sell his farm without his express permission.[18] Any tenant who wished to sell his interest in his holding, was required also to pay a year's rent as a fine and the new tenant was required to do the same. Whenever he thought the circumstances appropriate, Abercorn was able to remit this entry fine to either the buyer or the seller of the lease but he would not delegate this power to any of the agents. He often refused to accept as tenants outsiders who could not prove their potential. Although decision-making on the estate was slowed by this requirement, Abercorn's insistence ensured that no tenant could claim that he was ignorant about this pre-condition and it became recognised practice.

SUBLETTING

Abercorn was equally determined to control subdivision and subletting on his estate. Sub-letting probably carried the greater threat to the social development of the estate, especially when lessees who did not intend to occupy a farm themselves, parcelled it out among poor cottiers who had not the resources to make significant improvements. In 1745 McClintock reported to Abercorn that John Pearson had purchased lands; he was 'in no condition to hold them but by setting them to a parcel of cottiers who will be a continual pest to their neighbours and I don't believe he will be brought to do justice but by using the most severe methods with him'.[19] Although Pearson had not the resources to exploit this practice, there were others who had. In 1753 Nisbitt related the latest such exploit of one of them:

> I am informed Alexander Cochran has also purchased from George Barclay [for £400] John Harvey's lease of Lower Castleton; he pretends this also is for his son; I told Cochran that your Lordship consented his son should have the parts of Upper Castleton he lately purchased, provided he did not put cottiers in it, but live there himself; he said he would not put cottiers in it, though I am pretty sure it will be the case, as he has no married son, and Upper and Lower Castleton would be too large a farm for any man in the country. I think it my duty to inform your Lordship that the planting of cottiers is too common in the manor of Magavelin for as those kind of people are all tenants at will, they make no improvement and any little that is made wherever they come, they destroy it , and ruin your Lordship's turf bogs, which is a thing will be much wanted in time, in many places. I told Cochran I believed your Lordship would not suffer one man to purchase a number of farms for he has a large holding in Dundee [townland] too, which he purchased before I was agent and set to cottiers'.[20]

Abercorn responded: 'If it is true that Cochran has bought Harvey's farm in Castleton too, tell him I expect he settles some one good tenant upon each of them by November, and that I will not confirm any tenant right that he shall give anybody to them after that time, nor consider himself as having any.'[21] This decision maintained Abercorn's control over the development of the farm.

The problem was complicated further in 1769 when Abercorn discovered what he considered to be an unjust irregularity. Abercorn was prepared to countenance the employment of cottiers on a farm as 'necessary workmen' but he would not accept that undertenants who had occupied land for thirty-three years at rent as high as £26, should be treated as cottiers with no security of tenure.[22] Jemmy Hamilton found it difficult to understand why

Abercorn was so excited: 'Almost every tenant has a cottier: in most cases it's hard for them to want a labourer. If it was not I think they would not venture, as they have found your Lordship often established them.'[23] Nevertheless, when the opportunity occurred Abercorn insisted that Jemmy should tackle one of the tenants, Robert Harper of Listymore. Jemmy read

> the paragraph out of your Lordship's letter relating to him over and over again, to show him how absolutely necessary it was for him to give his undertenants a full security of the parts they have. I asked him if he would not think it hard if he had in every respect during his lease behaved as a good tenant ought, to be turned out at the expiration of it and not get it on any terms. He said he would but he thought the cases were not the same, for that at the time he had set to those people [he had said] that he must have it for his own family at the end of their term and bound them in a pretty large penalty to give it up peaceably. He argued much about it and said he did nothing but what his neighbours did. I told him I was sure it would be the same with all. Then he said no person would venture to bring in even a labourer, which would greatly prevent the improvement of your Lordship's estates. Indeed he insisted on that very strenuously.[24]

A petition from Harper did not alter Abercorn's resolution. Abercorn was determined to enforce covenants in the lease as firmly as tenants did on their undertenants: at the same time he did not wish the undertenants to jump to the conclusion that they had acquired tenant right by the transaction.[25]

In the end Harper had to concede with bad grace. Jemmy told Abercorn that Harper 'came to tell me that his wife was ready to break her heart about it and said the farm would be too small for their family; yet he then and before told me he would hold to the agreement if your Lordship approved of it'.[26] Before the year was out, however, Harper had sold his farm and taken his family to America.

In another case Jemmy provided more information about the background to this form of subletting:

> It is plain by all their agreements that they guard against that, for they set five or six years short of the tenure they have. Beside, they bind them under a penalty, and sometimes by oath, to give up peaceably when their term is expired and that they are not to petition or otherwise apply for any tenant right. Was I to lean to either side it would be to that of the under-tenant who generally labours with great industry, and pays exorbitantly for his earning and improves much more land I am sure than the immediate tenant, and if he was found on the land at the end of the lease I would wish him to be continued. But if he bargains

and obliges himself to give it up, I think his pretension is the less. The case of such is certainly hard: they must, if not by the merest chance they become tenants themselves, go on with much hardship and lose the fruits of their labour . . .

Many of your Lordship's farms as well as Listymore have rough tracts that want active hands, as your Lordship observes. Your Lordship will I hope pardon my taking the liberty of saying that I apprehend that the improvement will be more where the tenant may avowedly set off parts for some years than when it is otherwise, for he might think it best to hold all though he cannot manage it, than to run a risk of losing part of it.[27]

He emphasised his point soon afterwards by retailing a conversation:

I lately heard a poor man say that had brought in one of the tenants thence, that it was the worst thing that ever could happen to the poor, this application to your Lordship from the under-tenants or cottiers, and upon my asking him his reason, he sayed that to be sure that the tenants would not venture hereafter, to set off any part of their lands, and what would become of such as him that had no land.[28]

On this estate it would appear that this episode marked the final stage in the creation of a distinction between the under-tenant class and the cottier class. In future tenants would not venture to sub-lease any part of their lands to under-tenants. The more ambitious of the under-tenants would be driven either to purchase small-holdings as they came on the market or to lease marginal lands for reclamation. Cottiers would hold only at the will of the tenant-farmer and be liable to eviction at any time.

Jemmy Hamilton linked this struggle to the incidence of emigration on the estate in 1772 when he reported to the earl:

A vast number have gone to America this season but very few comparatively from your Lordship's estates, having excellent bargains and protected every way in their rights; nor can they pretend to have the smallest cause to grumble, unless those who may consider it a hardship that their tenants should be continued with them longer than their term, and this can only proceed from your Lordship's tenderness for the poor people under them. I would not presume to mention this, but that I find some discontented about it . . . [29]

This comment is a reminder that many emigrants who left Ireland retailing stories of injustice at the hands of landlords and agents, could not have proved their cases before a judge.

Two letters prove that Jemmy was still pressing his arguments about this matter on Abercorn in the closing years of their partnership. By that time, however, two interesting changes of emphasis in his letters had surfaced. Resistance was strengthening in the management of the estate against the further subdivision or 'splitting' of farms. Jemmy was able also to present a case stressing the positive aspects of the relationship between tenant and cottier:

> I do think it would be more for the advantage of the estates that tenants were allowed to let skirts of their farms without fearing to lose the tenant right of it, and to avoid splitting as much as possible. The cottier in such cases would be helped by his landlord. He would give him assistance in many ways; he would give him weaving and labour to enable him to pay his rent; they would get leases for perhaps ten years; they would live as friends, whereas the tenant who would get a mountainy bit, your Lordship's tenant who considers the farm all his right is seldom friendly to the little tenant who lives on a part he intended for a son in a future day.[30]
>
> There are many cottiers who pay from 10s. to 15s. in very much more distress than those who pay much more than double to a tenant who keeps the cottier's house thatched, brings home his turf, puts out his manure, serves him with meal or potatoes in his distress, and in general takes work for all. I really think I can observe the tenant's farm who has a working cottier in better order than his neighbours who has not one.[31]

The whole tone of the references to cottiers on the Abercorn estates in these letters is more positive than the picture presented by John McEvoy in the *Statistical survey of the county of Tyrone* (1802) and remind us that because individual estates had devised certain solutions to widespread social problems and developed singular characteristics, they should not be viewed as micro-cosms of provincial or national society.

SUBDIVISION

In the early stages of the plantation the owners of estates granted the best leases to authoritative individuals who were prepared to be answerable both for the regular payment of the rent and duties and the performance of the covenants in the leases. Such tenants were required to take responsibility for the payment of rent by each of the subtenants. On other estates where such individuals were in short supply an alternative strategy was to bind groups of tenants together in a lease, holding them jointly responsible for the payment of the rent. In time, however, more colonist families were prepared to accept the responsibility of a lease which brought them into a direct relationship with the landlord and recognised their status within the community. By the mid-eighteenth century native families also were taking leases for terms of twenty-one or thirty-one years: until the 1793 Relief Act a Catholic tenant was not permitted to hold land by a lease for lives. These terms of leases should enable us to distinguish between Catholic and Protestant tenants on an estate during this period.

The family was a powerful force especially when it united to fight against external threats but it was also a generator of fierce internal quarrels. Both Abercorn and Jemmy would have agreed with the sentiments of Montaigne: 'There is scarcely any less bother in the running of a family than in that of an entire state. And domestic business is no less importunate for being less important.'[32] The major problem was that the wealth of many families was bound up in their farms and it was very difficult for farmers, unlike weavers, to realise their assets when they needed cash. As Jemmy pointed out to his master: 'These debts that become burdens on the farms are very ruinous. If the daughter at her marriage does not get a bit of the farm, her portion is borrowed and becomes in the end a demand on the farm. They seldom make any other provision for son and daughter than the land'.[33] On the death of the leaseholder, too, it often proved very difficult to secure agreement on the division of his property. Among the most substantial elements of the correspondence between Abercorn and Jemmy in the final quarter of the century, family problems loomed large and they were expected to provide a solution even when they had had no hand in the making of the will. Indeed, much of their problem seems to have stemmed from the care they took and their initial successes. In cases of this kind the term *rundale* was used to denote land that was held in common between two or more people, usually after the death of a leaseholder. The rarity of rundale surviving the renewal of a lease is revealed by Jemmy Hamilton's reaction to the novel problem he faced when required to describe the holding in Lower Phedeyglass that Alexander Lowry held in rundale with his brother James: he sent both the lease and its counterpart to Abercorn.[34] In a subsequent letter he explained to Abercorn that 'there was not a blank large enough in the lease for expressing in a proper manner the half of Lower Phedeyglass'.[35]

Making divisions between tenants during the term of a lease had long been viewed as a difficult process by the estate management because tenants could not be forced to accept the decisions of any third party. In 1754 Abercorn had instructed his then agent, Nathaniel Nisbitt:

> I would have you employ a surveyor when the weather is good to make divisions where they are wanted. They must bear as near a proportion

as conveniently may be to the respective holdings of the tenants, but need not correspond so exactly as where lands are already in lease. By making the divisions now the tenants will have two years trial of them, and may have the advantage of being relieved in any hardships that may happen.[36]

This tone was maintained in another letter from Abercorn to Nisbitt in 1758:

You will see by the map that the divisions of [the townland of] Cavandoragh are extremely awkward owing perhaps to an observance of the divisions the tenants had made themselves. I only desire in general to have it better divided into two or more parts, so as none of it may remain to be held in common. And as there is great complaint of damage done by a variety of roads through it to the mountain bog, I desire to have at the same time one or two roads laid out to it, which all persons must keep to.[37]

As time passed the problem became even more common and Jemmy in 1767 asked Abercorn to provide a set of regulations that the tenants could accept:

There are few divisions made by the tenants themselves that they abide by though bound by article and sometimes by oath. Sometimes they agree that one of themselves should divide and give the other a choice for some consideration in money; sometimes that it is divided [by] indifferent persons and cast lots for the part each is to have. When one complains, the other produces his article to show he keeps to it. Another would say he would change with his neighbour but that he is sworn to abide by the division he has got. Divisions are for the tenants' interest but in general it is impossible to prevail on them to abide by them, nor should the person complaining show good reason for having some alteration made, will the other allow it. Divisions are the causes of most of the disputes and would therefore hope your lordship would give some orders concerning them.[38]

Abercorn soon responded:

As you desire me to make some regulation about the division of farms, I do direct that any tenants desirous of a division, may put their leases into your hands, under assurance of having them restored when the division shall be made under my order, without any advance or expence to them of any sort, and as conveniently may be. And I will support no division made after by themselves . . .[39]

Not long after this decision, however, Jemmy began to sound a warning note about the threat posed by the urge for dividing holdings. Families who subdivided their holdings might satisfy the individuals concerned but they were undermining the status of the family in society and rendering it more vulnerable during a downturn in the economy.

> It is scarce possible to prevent the tenants from dividing their land. Dorlan of Dunrevan's father who petitioned your Lordship for the bit he gave to his grandson, your Lordship left tenant at £3. 8s. 6d.; there are now three on that part and each must have a horse and have some little business to do in the land, and I am convinced that had one kept it, or rather a larger farm, supposing he paid a full value, that he would be abler to pay than if he had one of those parts for nothing.
>
> John Mathers of Tavnabreen desired I should press James Wilson to divide the part with him that they bought from John Marshall. The reason that Mathers wants it is that if it was thrown into his farm that possibly it might be continued to him at the renewal, and Wilson refuses dividing hoping that it may be returned to the part he holds. It's going on for the remainder of the lease in rundale can be but little inconvenience. Then your Lordship will judge to whom it ought to go.[40]

The same policy was followed in settling boundary disputes with neighbouring estates. It was important to settle disputes as quickly as possible to prevent them from escalating into confrontation. Meetings were held between knowledgeable representatives who had the confidence of management and they interrogated the oldest inhabitants to find out the location of the boundaries and their marking stones.

NEGOTIATING RENT

Those who believe that tenants were poorly informed about the circumstances of other tenants will be surprised by the contents of this letter:

> The tenants of Lower Loughnea with much seeming difficulty offered to pay £33, they say they took it much too high and that they were promised abatement by John Hamilton but that he sold it and William never gave it them; I find they have had some country surveyor for they offered to pay the above rent or 12 shillings an acre, for all they hold except the bog, which is not they say pastureable or improveable; they seem to have an eye to the large abatement Upper Loughnea expected, for when I spoke of the inconsiderable advance they offered, compared to the other Loughneas, they told me their abatement would be £12

yearly; I wondered how they could pretend to guess at any thing; they said your Lordship used to name a rent, which if they were able they would pay; perhaps your Lordship would think best to name the rents to me and I would try them.[41]

By the late 1780s, however, petitions against rent increases were being organised not by townlands but by parishes. There was also a different tone about them because they were being drawn up by professionals, such as this one on behalf of the tenants of the parishes of Donagheady and Leckpatrick:

Permit me, with all that respect which is due to your elevated station, to throw myself at your Lordship's feet on behalf of myself and other tenants of your Lordship in the parishes of Donagheady and Leck. My Lord, it is generally reported that an additional rent is to be laid upon your tenants. Now any further 'burthen' of this kind especially in the above-mentioned places, I can assure your Lordship, 'tis impossible for them to bear. The lands are already very dear, so that punishing want and poverty is staring many of us in the face and if they are again to be raised, God only knows what the consequences may be. The only prospect to great numbers (a dreary and comfortless prospect indeed) will be from their utter inability to pay the rent, either to be cast abroad in a starving situation to the world or to rot in the body of jail, or if so much is left as to waft us across the ocean, we may try to find some shelter in a foreign land. Gentlemen who have access to your Lordship's company, may in conversation (and to this we fear our hardships are greatly owing) represent that your lands are still cheap and capable of an additional rise but indeed, my Lord, the case is quite otherwise. Such representations are given by these men from interested views either to ingratiate themselves into favour, or who being themselves in affluent circumstances, feel not for the necessity of the poor. Basking in the sunshine of prosperity and rolling in wealth they consider not the situation of the indigent and distressed, wretched insensibility that makes men callous to the distress of their fellow brethren around and regardless of what may befall them in ensuring themselves are happy and well. How strange that that rule so excellent, that rule of eternal and universal obligation of doing to others as we would wish to be done to us, should be so far forgotten. It may be alleged (as we fear it frequently is) as a strong proof of your lands being set at a moderate value that considerable sums of money are given by purchasers to those who dispose of their farms. These sums, however, my Lord, are given solely with a view to obtain a residence in the country. Naturally attached to the country which gave us birth, we pay extravagant sums, sums procured by labour and industry, rather than remove to a strange land, and leave the society of our friends and neighbours. Indeed, if the purchasers of these farms after their being settled in them became rich or wealthy then there would be an undeniable proof of their being cheap but if the contrary is the case, if the purchasers with all their care and industry, all their parsimony and economy, is with the utmost difficulty able to support their families and pay the rent, then surely it cannot be fairly argued that they are cheaper. Could I represent to your Lordship the situation of numbers of your tenantry, honest, sober and industrious men, I am persuaded that compassion would wring your heart for their distress. If your Lordship could take an excursion among them without being known to observe their manner of living, the beds on which they are obliged to repose at night, the homely and oft scanty meals to which they must sit down after the painful labour and toils of the day, the poor clothing to defend themselves and children from the inclemencies of the weather, I am persuaded that instead of augmenting you would rather think of lowering their rents. Be not displeased, my Lord, with my freedom in thus representing things as they really are. I am pleading the cause of humanity and am not without hopes of being attended to.[42]

A fortnight later Jemmy reported to the earl: 'I have had a good many of the Donelong tenants with me to agree for their land. The complaint I may say was general – quite too dear; we may hold it for a year or two; talked a good deal but still settled . . . '.[43] On 9 March he recounted: 'A great number of the Cloghogle tenants met on Friday at Leck[patrick] church. Mr Rouse on his return from holding a court in the manor of Donelong saw a great many of them and told them they were very absurd. I heard that they collected pence apiece from as many as would give it to them, to give to an attorney to draw up a petition to send to your Lordship.'[44] The petition submitted to the earl from the tenants of the manor of Donelong, very similar in content to the earlier one, is dated 1 April 1788. On 20 April Jemmy commented:

> The tenants come in very slowly to settle for their rents. Even those who have paid November 1786 rent don't come in. I do believe that the hopes of a general abatement prevents many of them . . . As the people all know the rent that is expected, I suppose they judge that their holding back will be attended with no loss. There have been but 18 counterparts yet perfected. One of the persons who signed his counterpart said he would sign it for he was sure your Lordship would abate him if you abated the rest. He said he heard that your Lordship was to let them hold for eleven years at their old rents and that he was told I had got orders to that purpose.[45]

After working together for more than two decades Jemmy and the earl had reached the degree of unanimity expressed in this letter written by Jemmy to him in 1785. No-one, however, could accuse him of failing to advocate the welfare of the tenants:

> There have been a good many changes of tenants but I am confident that there has not been one that was not for the good of the estate. In some instances they are not as I would wish, but in them only where the tenant could not hold all or a purchaser [be] got for more than half of the farm. There were others who could not hold all and would sell but the half, though the purchaser would have bought all: in that case they have entered into an article by which the purchaser engages to pay at the same rate for the other half, in case your Lordship would not allow it to be split. There can hardly be any instances where it is not hurtful to split farms. The larger the farms the surer the rent and in many cases where the farms have skirts not reclaimed, I do think it is for the good of the estate that the tenant is suffered to let them. In general the undertenant would be continued and though at a much higher rent than your Lordship would lay on it, yet the undertenant has employment from the tenant who lets to him; he has his favour and pays most of his rent in labour; at the same time his part is no doubt improving something.[46]

Occasionally in the correspondence there is sufficient information to compose case studies that afford us glimpses into the everyday world of the late eighteenth century Ulster estate. One such case is that of John McNeelans who held a farm of thirteen acres of marginal land in Shanoney West. On 11 June 1773 Jemmy Hamilton informed the earl that McNeelans 'who pays £2.15s. yearly rent in Shanoney ran away in debt chiefly to the tenants about £70', having borrowed clothes on the pretext of going to a fair. McNeelans's eighty year old mother said he would not return. The tenants, who had been expecting McNeelans to make a composition with them for his debts, allowed Jemmy to take the initiative in sorting out the mess. Before he left the first meeting, he made arrangements for the care of the old woman and agreed with a man to cut turf for the farm while the creditors who lived about the farm undertook to shovel the potatoes and take care of the crop. Jemmy asked the earl for permission to sell the remainder of the lease, reckoning that the sale of the interest and lease might fetch £30. The lease, however, belonged to the mother for, as the earl explained, the neighbours had objected to him getting a new lease in his own name. As everyone agreed that the lease should be sold, the earl was prepared to grant 'the supposed term' to a new tenant, ordering that the sale must pay off the arrears of rent plus a year's rent as an entry fine; then provision was to be made for the mother and the residue divided among the creditors. Jemmy thought the final task would be the most difficult because creditors could claim any figure and some were claiming even the ownership of crops on which they had lent McNeelans money. The tithe-farmer too entered 'a demand of five years including this crop which comes to £3.5s.' although he was prepared to be treated like the other creditors. To assist in the task of disentangling McNeelans's affairs, a message was sent to him living, as it was reported, about Ballyshannon, 'to send in an account in writing of what he fairly owes'. Several days later Jemmy was persuaded to adjourn the sale for nearly a fortnight 'by which time it's supposed McNeelans will come to settle his affairs as his creditors have given him two months licence.' More than a month elapsed, however, before Jemmy informed the earl: 'One Erwin, a brother-in-law of John McNeelans, bought his holding in Shanoney at £26. The old woman is to live with him.'[47]

Whereas Jemmy was able to settle the McNeelans's case inside four months with the co-operation of the tenants, the case of Edward French became a long-running drama mainly because of the earl's personal interest in French who had paid him a visit in London. In 10 July 1772 Jemmy gave the earl details of a dispute between James Kerr and his cottier Edward French [or Francis: both surnames appear in the correspondence]. Because French had gone to see his Lordship, Jemmy had difficulty in dissuading Kerr from going also. Kerr declared that he would give French anything, 'treble what his improvements are worth, if he would leave him', while claiming that French destroyed his grain and pestered and bullied him and his family.[48] Abercorn, however, must have been impressed by his visitor for he instructed Jemmy to look after French's family on the estate. On 25 July 1772 Jemmy replied with a trace of irony: 'I received French's family and will supply them, if I find them in distress, but his being away at this time may not distress them, for probably he will labour in England and his family I am told often beg at this season of the year, which very many now do, who are much better able to support themselves . . .'.[49] Only a week later, however, Jemmy had to report:

> I found three of French's family ill in the smallpox, and the mother kept at home attending on them; I gave her a crown which was great relief to her, and told her to call on me when she came to market. On Tuesday she came for meal and told me that one of the children was dead; she asked me whether your Lordship had ordered me to give her money. I did not directly say that I had got orders, lest after she knew it she might not be easily contented; I asked her if she stood in need of anything then, as she had her child to bury; she declined taking any but said she would see me next Tuesday.[50]

Further misfortune was to follow for French at the end of September when Edward Kerr used the law to dispossess him. Jemmy reported to Abercorn:

> When I went there I found Kerr and Francis's wife and others; I taxed him with his having broken his promise to me, for when I got your Lordship's letter desiring me to defend Francis by law, I sent for Kerr and read him the paragraph, and laid before him the consequences of his persisting; he wept prodigiously and said he would again lay his case before your Lordship, and solemnly promised he would drop any proceedings at law, and as the term was over, I knew he could have none till November.[51]

Kerr, however, reiterated in very strong terms that he would not allow any of the family to stay there until the harvest was over and Jemmy had to get them into a good house belonging to Pat Diven of Liskey. 'Francis's wife tells me they owe over and above the year's rent £4.10s. and some tithe which they must pay Kerr and about £9 to others'.

When Kerr prevented Mrs Francis from removing goods from her old home, Jemmy 'told him . . . that I would drive him for a third penny more rent, as his lease directed; he bid me do so if I pleased, for if I stripped him of all he had on earth, he would be content, but that Francis should not live in the same townland with him, if I was to lay him down five hundred pounds.'[52] When Kerr refused to let Francis remove his crops unless he paid him £18 for rent and tithes and the cost of the ejectment, Jemmy had to visit Kerr again and negotiate for the crops. By this time both Kerr and French were intransigent[53] but Abercorn merely told Jemmy: 'I am obliged to you for taking care of French. You must continue to do so. As there are not many years of Kerr's lease, I shall decline entering into a law suit with him. There is nothing more for me to say but that I refuse my consent to Kerr's selling his lease.'[54]

A few days later Jemmy reported: 'I saw French last week; his wife is ill of a fever; I have given her £1. 5s. 5½d. which as he purposes paying, I did not charge; he tells me that Diven wants the house he lives in, that he would try to exchange his holding in Shanoney with some of the tenants; that the McCrossans of Doneyglade are his relations, that probably some of them might change with him, but that he would not meddle in it till I heard something about it from your Lordship. I had his corn drawn in and stacked with James Hill in Drumahoe'.[55] By 15 November Jemmy had promised Francis that he would try to get him a place on the estate of his own brother Claud Hamilton at Gortin, but he had to admit that Francis had 'very little to settle anywhere with'.[56]

Within a fortnight French's cottier house in Shanoney had been burned to the ground and so there was no prospect of the family returning to it. Mrs

French refused to move from Diven's house until Hamilton got her another 'which will not be easily procured, as the people find it so difficult to remove them'. Jemmy also failed to get him into his brother's estate.[57]

> French has not got anyone to exchange for the holding he had in Shanoney; one reason to be sure is that a holding directly under your lordship, of half the rent that French paid, would be better than his; he is much distressed for a place, nor can I find a way of fixing him; the people don't like him and dread letting him in; I was told that a first cousin of his had agreed to accomodate him, and that he removed some potatoes to it, and that now he will not have him.[58]

A few months later Jemmy learned that French had moved to Strabane and must have realised that he would be pestered even more often by French and his wife who appeared to believe that the agent's role was to sort out their problems and satisfy their needs. French had taken an empty tenement in Irish Street and begun to repair it. 'His wife called to me this day for money, and when I told her I could not give her any, she was very angry and said she would apply to your Lordship.'[59]

Even Jemmy had to admit that French was working hard to some effect although he resented having to lend him small sums of money at short notice: 9s. 2½d. to pay for straws to his house and £1. 0s. 4d. worth of timber that was blown down near the town. He earned himself a reprimand from the earl when he suggested: 'I will if your Lordship pleases take his bond, as he is not anyhow able to pay at present, though he will work himself into something'.[60] The earl's reply was: 'French's little debt is by no means the object of a bond'.[61]

Time passed and the final reference to Edward French in the correspondence appears to have been written by the agent, tongue in cheek:

> Edward French who lived cottier once with James Kerr of Shanoney and who, I believe, went twice to your Lordship to London, is greatly in debt; his wife happened to be in a fever while he was in London and your Lordship ordered me to help to support her and her family; I think she got about £5 from time to time which your Lordship allowed me; I took his bond for that, the arrears he owed in November 1777 in Patrick Street and £10 he undertook to pay for No 39, a field William Dougherty held and had run away from, amounting in all to £28. 18s. 9d. and I know no possibility of getting any of it unless I enter judgment on his bond and sell the houses he built in Patrick Street; he is a poor hardworking man, yet in debt beside this; he has run away from this or absconded to try to settle with his creditors; his wife keeps in one of the houses; indeed it's mostly locked up while she is abegging;

she has nothing in her house; when I ask for her husband she tells me she does not know where he is; perhaps he's in London, that I need not be uneasy about what he owes, for she hopes he will get more from your Lordship.[62]

Both these cases provide vivid accounts of the problems faced by poor people struggling to make a living on this estate and the strategies they used to survive. While the earl was in a position to indulge a tenant, the agent had to be consistent in his behaviour towards all the tenants. He knew only too well from bitter experience that his conduct was always under the scrutiny of the tenants and kindnesses could provide opportunities for others to exploit.

Improving the Estate

Now that the Irish great estate has passed into history it is very difficult from the viewpoint of the present day to understand the significant role that it played, especially in Ulster society, and to appreciate the functions that it performed for its members. The glory of the great houses and demesnes with their gardens and monuments obscure the real contribution that the estate network made to the development of its community.

The estate belonged to the landlord and in the printed leases that became commonplace in the late eighteenth century he inserted specific clauses to reserve

> all manner of mines, minerals, quarries of freestone, limestone, slate, and coals, all woods, underwoods, timber and trees, of all kinds whatsoever, all turf bogs, mosses and marl, together with all royalties whatsoever; with full and free liberty to and for the said [landlord's name], his heirs and assigns, into the said demised premises to enter and there search for, dig up, cut down and carry away any of the aforesaid royalties, at any time or times during this demise, at the will and pleasure of him the said [landlord's name], his heirs and assigns.[1]

To preserve these resources and control access to the bogs and woods, the estate employed moss bailiffs and wood-rangers. Searches were made by miners recruited from Britain for mines and quarries that might be leased to tenants to exploit.

Throughout the estate the Abercorn administration provided essential services for the tenants by promoting and supervising markets and fairs, constructing and repairing roads and bridges, maintaining corn mills, building and supplying kilns for producing lime, organising turbary and the raising of bog timber, protecting fisheries, and supervising ferries across the Foyle and its tributaries. The earl persevered with his ambition to provide Strabane with a commodious harbour entered by way of a canal from the river Foyle but construction was not undertaken before his death and so his successor reaped all the plaudits. Towards the close of the earl's life, too, the decision was taken to plant forests around the demesne on a very large scale similar to that at Lord Mountjoy's estate near Omagh. All the time the agents were encouraging tenants to enclose their fields, reclaim marginal land, and improve their farming methods.

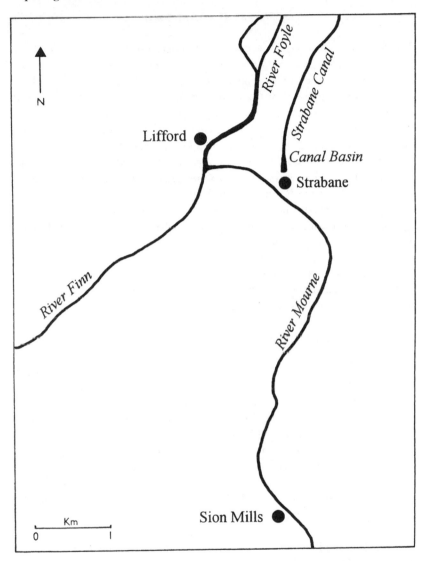

2. Strabane and Lifford

THE STRABANE CANAL PROJECT

The Strabane Canal (fig. 2) was constructed between 1791 and 1796, not by the eighth earl but by his nephew who succeeded him in 1789 and was raised to the dignity of marquess in 1790. The very success of the canal has somehow deprived the eighth earl of the credit for initiating the whole project and driving it forward. In 1774 he had written to one of his agents, John Hamilton in Strabane: 'The improvement of the navigation of the northern part of the county of Tyrone, is an object that, as you know, I have long had in view.'[2]

Although the town of Strabane lay along the River Mourne, there was no site for a landing place and so was born the idea of cutting a canal that would enable boats from the River Foyle to bring cargoes into the town itself. In 1757 Michael Preistley began to mark out the ground for the canal, taking advantage of canals or cuts made near the town by an earlier surveyor, William Starrat, to drain the bogland.[3]

There is nothing in the correspondence to suggest why this scheme was not completed. The next mention of the canal project was not until some eleven years had passed and John Hamilton was pressed by the townspeople to raise the matter with the earl. He explained the arguments advanced by the tenants:

> The Parliament often grants money for works not so useful as this would be, for if the canal was completed, I doubt not but this town might be made a discharging port. At the time your Lordship made that canal, the stuff was chiefly pulled up by grapples, as it would not stand cutting with spades, but now the sides are firm, and by my best advice, as much might now be done for one third of the then expence. There is one Ducart employed in this county and in many other parts of the kingdom, in carrying on such works; if your Lordship would think fit to order him to make an estimate of it and permit it to be laid before the Parliament, we would hope for assistance; pardon me my Lord for pretending in this matter but really the inhabitants have pressed me much to write about this affair.[4]

The earl consulted his relative, William Brownlow, the member of parliament for County Armagh, whose reply was not encouraging:

> A great deal of the sort of work your Lordship mentions has been carried on, or rather attempted in this country, but with so little success, and at the same time at so heavy an expence, that I should not be fond of employing any that had been concerned in them; we have had a variety of engineers and every new one has discovered many blunders in his predecessor, but has generally entailed at least as many on his successors; the favourite at present is a Piedmontese; his name is Du

Carte; he dropped into this kingdom from the clouds, no one knows how, or what brought him to it; he was first employed in the south as an architect, and acquitted himself to the satisfaction of his employers; for three or four years past he has been engaged in lines of navigation and approved of; he now directs the works in the county of Tyrone near Stewartstown and on that account may be induced to undertake the direction of the work at Strabane at more moderate terms; he is certainly an excellent draughtsman, and taker of levels, and is indefatigable in anything he undertakes; he was under examination as to lines and levels last winter before a committee of the House of Commons and what I saw of him there gave me a good impression of him. I shall write to him . . .

This seems to me what will best answer your Lordship's intention, for I would by no means recommend any of those who have learned their trade under Owen or any of the other engineers whose blunders we have experenced, but I should imagine if your Lordship could get anyone trained under Brindley or Smeaton, you would have a better chance of success, at less expense; I know their names are in such high esteem here that the opinion of one of their journeymen would be more attended to than the greatest master in this country.[5]

Brownlow did correspond with Davis Dukart and enclosed in his own letter to the earl, a letter from Dukart detailing his charges.[6] The earl passed the letter to John Hamilton who was clearly shaken by Abercorn's initiative:

I am honoured with yours respecting Mr Dukart's inspection of our navigation which I am confident was never thought of by any but your Lordship and us of this place, nor did I mean more when I mentioned a parliamentary grant, than the completing the canal to this town, as there are large sums often given upon much less reasonable grounds; besides I am assured by the most judicious people here, that should this navigation be continued up the River Mourne, the canal through the bog will be found the easiest and most adviseable course, so that should we obtain aid from parliament, it could never be deemed the result of any private scheme.

As to the extending the navigation up the River Mourne, it is thought by us almost impracticable on account of the nature of the river, which has many shoals and vastly rocky in many parts, nor is there that trade upwards that would encourage such an undertaking for most of the inhabitants above Omagh go to Newry for their goods. It would give all your Lordship's people here real concern to think our prospects might be absorbed in a great scheme which probably never will be executed. If Mr Dukart finds (which we believe will be the case) that the bog is the proper course should a navigation above Strabane be thought of, then we would hope for aid from Parliament upon proper application. Lord Erne no doubt would be for the river to Lifford, as would the different interests hope to have it extended to Castlefin, but there are three shoals between Desert and Lifford not passable but on spring tides, which if cleared, we are sure would be filled with floods. If the canal is made from Desert through the bog to Strabane, it will be the most effectual way to make this place flourish.[7]

Another four years or so passed before the townspeople submitted a memorial which Jemmy transmitted to the earl with his comments

> At the desire of the principal traders I enclose your Lordship a memorial. The great delay of boats occasioned chiefly by the shallows between Lifford and Greenlaw, on account of which they sometimes bring out such things there as men can carry to where horses can come, at considerable expence beside great loss by the boatmen, who when they are long detained on the water, drink and dispose of their liquors and other things to the people on the shores. There are many complaints and inquiries of things lost or so disposed of.
>
> One of the merchants told me that he had lately a boat with wines and other liquors that had been twenty-eight days in coming from Derry and that he believed he lost in that time £20 worth. There are other shallows between Greenlaw and Donelong. Could they be avoided vessels of considerable burthen might, I am told, come up, but those seldom interrupt small boats, as they can be got over by any tide.
>
> The land carriage is mostly from below Lifford where there is a quay at which each boat pays a shilling, when they put in at this side of the water there is there also some expense. They can not but in flood time bring a boat to the strand at Lifford bridge. When they put in a little below that, those who have not agreed by the year, pay according to the loads they bring up.
>
> The land carriage and the expence attending it is no great consideration at present but if certain water carriage could be had, there is reason to think that this place would still flourish.

MEMORIAL

> That the canal begun by your Lordship some years ago gave us hopes that in time there might be a navigable communication open between this town and the river which would have in a great measure put us upon a footing with our importing neighbours of Derry as we have some advantage over them in the land carriage of goods from Dublin. Our situation in the midst of a cultivated country is well adapted for a very extensive

trade which has too apparently been on the decline these many years, but certainly would be revived and greatly promoted, could a canal be obtained.[8]

While the earl's inclination had been for a canal into Strabane because that would have allowed him to take all the decisions, he knew that such a project depended on the abandonment of the alternative scheme to make the River Mourne navigable as far as Omagh. He needed this scheme put to the test and so he told Jemmy: 'As for the money that has been spent upon the sort of canal that there is already, I am very willing to consider it as so much lost, or rather given to the poor in a time of dearth. That will therefore lay no restraint upon any ideas the surveyor may have. I only wish he may not be sent for until they are fully prepared what to say to him.'[9] When the matter was raised again in mid-January the following year he instructed his agents, the Hamilton brothers, to let it be known

> as occasion shall happen to offer, that I am ready to subscribe £12,000 for that purpose; so, nevertheless, as my subscription do not exceed one third part of the whole sum subscribed. This I wish to be understood rather as an intimation of my desire to follow what may be the sense of other gentlemen, than as a proposal coming from me, in which I mean to take a lead.[10]

By proposing to support any decision that the principal gentlemen of the county might reach, the earl had forced them to declare themselves about the navigation and they were not sufficiently impressed to undertake the scheme.

The earl was amused by the report of the meeting at which Ducart had set out to impress the audience and ended by killing the scheme stone dead:

> I thought the principal gentlemen of Tyrone would, perhaps, enter into a scheme for carrying on a navigation towards Omagh, if the expense of it should be found likely to be moderate, and that nothing would more probably induce them to it than the appointment of an engineer chosen by themselves, whom they would have an opportunity of instructing and limiting within such bounds of expense as the circumstances of the county might be supposed to render necessary. But the part Dukart has taken could only tend to make them laugh and to defeat the project entirely, whilst he thought he was merely giving a specimen of his genius and imagination. Navigation to Omagh upon his largest scale would cost the county perhaps half a million.[11]

When the Strabane canal project was revived by his successor there was no further mention of the Mourne project. The new canal, more than four miles in length with two locks, was capable of taking ocean-going schooners of more than three hundred tons burden.[12] Of course, these vessels would have had to pass through, not under, the new timber bridge at Londonderry built by an American firm in 1790, and to run the gauntlet of their Derry rivals:

> Last week Pat Fleming, one of our principal merchants, had his boat at Derry quay laden to come here but could have no passage as there was no open arch. The people of Derry pressed the boatman to cut his mast but he chose rather to send to his owner who immediately went down, served a notice on the mayor as directed by the act, in consequence of which he got free passage and the boat came through full sail and flying colours to be sure.[13]

The Strabane canal proved a real asset to the flourishing market town until the construction of the Londonderry & Enniskillen Railway in the 1850s severely undermined its financial position.

ROADMAKING AND BRIDGEBUILDING

Perhaps the greatest contribution to the Irish economy by landlords in the late eighteenth century was their organisation of the great programme of roadbuilding that transformed the countryside. Ireland had inherited the English practice of devolving the construction and maintenance of roads on the parish vestry but the annual programme of six days' labour was inadequate to cope with cross-country routes that were vital for the development of commerce. That carriers were making regular trips from Strabane to Dublin in 1746 is confirmed from Jo. Colhoun's comment to the earl: 'The merchants of this town commonly pay in the winter six shillings per hundred [weight] from Dublin to Strabane, and in the summer five shillings and sometimes less for goods carried by the carrs.'[14]

An act of 1710[15] had extended the authority of grand juries to spend money on the repair and construction of roads where the six days' labour was insufficient to cope with the scale of the problem but the grand juries did not have the capital to finance such schemes. We know from various sources that major roads were being constructed in several counties and that some individuals were contributing money in lieu of the six days' labour.[16] Correspondence between the earl and his agents indicates that in the county of Tyrone, too, Abercorn was encouraging the agents to continue with road construction, especially in connection with his new market-town at Magheracreggan. In August 1750 he instructed Jo. Colhoun: 'When you write, let me know what has been done to the roads, and also how much of the road between Newtownstewart and Omagh is finished, and what is doing at Bunshanbo bridge'.[17] At the end of November in the same year the earl tackled Nisbitt in the same vein: 'P.S. If nothing is done to the roads in the parish of Urney, especially that from Strabane Bridge towards Ardstraw, pray speak to Dr Henry [the rector] and some of the principal inhabitants in my name and desire they will think of a proper overseer, and lay a scheme for setting to work early in the spring.'[18] In 1751 the earl instructed Colhoun:

> I would have McCrea [the surveyor] send me a plan of the new road from my limestone quarry to Magheracreggan, distinguishing the mile-stones and the houses upon it, and I would also have a plan of the little square at Magheracreggan where the market is kept. Kinkead should lay out all this year's money upon the road to the new bridge. I would have the new road made of the same breadth as the other to Magheracreggan and I believe three yards must be sufficient for the stoning.[19]

The acceptable minimum road width was increased from nine feet in 1710 to twelve feet in 1727 and to twenty-one feet for existing roads and thirty feet between fences for new roads in 1759, of which at least fourteen feet had to be gravelled.[20]

In April 1752 the earl reminded Colhoun: 'The time for making roads is drawing near. The best direction I can give for the manor of Derrygoon is to complete the road to the new bridge and repair the road to Magheracreggan *as far as the money will go*, rather than think of making any new work.'[21] The active roll that the estate was playing in the construction and maintenance of roads is defined in a letter from Jemmy Hamilton to the earl: 'When Mr Nisbitt gave me your Lordship's rent roll, he directed me to receive from the tenants of Derrygoon, at the rate of six [pence] a pound, for the repair of roads; I placed it accordingly in my half year's book by which I received. The tenants of Largeybeg think they are exempt from the payment of it, which I did not insist on till I knew your Lordship's orders.'[22] In his next letter Jemmy wrote:

> The road money shall be collected as your Lordship has directed, but would wish to know if there is any particular road your Lordship would order to be forwarded this ensuing season; the repairs that are to be made in Derrygoon on the road between Magheracreggan and Newtownstewart will be very inconsiderable but there is scarce any-thing done at the road between Drumquin and Ardstraw bridge, from the place it crosses Magheracreggan road. At last assize I applied for a presentment for making a new road from Magheracreggan towards Killeter, which was granted, £25 to be raised against next assize and £25 at the assize following; the people of Magheracreggan spoke to me about it and told me that it would be of infinite advantage, which appeared to me plainly when I examined the road now laid out, which is shorter by the half (and more) than the road they have hitherto had.

> I shall endeavour as your Lordship desires, to have the Largeybeg tenants six days labour applied where it will be of most service to them.[23]

The Largeybeg tenants may have been exempt from paying road money but they were required instead to perform their six days labour on the roads: it would have been supervised well. Even if parishioners preferred to pay road money rather than provide six days of labour on the roads, they knew that it had become a charge on their holdings and that they would not be able to evade its exaction. The agents would collect the road money, charged at six-pence in the pound of rent, and spend it locally according to the requirements of the estate. Jemmy's letter explains the new procedure:

> When your Lordship ordered that the road money should be received yearly at May, I made out a list, the copy of which I gave John Kinkead, with the sums due by each denomination for a year and a half at May 1758, with a column for payments which I examined last week and find that he received not quite £8 as above; the people have promised the bailiff to meet me at Magheracreggan Fair on Friday and pay it off. There is expended in stoning and gravelling the road, raising the sunk bridge and filling it with stone and gravel repairing several pipes and Magheralough Bridge: £10. 4s. For making several repairs and mending part of Bunshamboe Bridge: £5. 19s. 7½d. John Kinkead's wages for his care for a year: £2. 5s. 6d. Cash expended: £18. 9s. 1½ d.[24]

Jemmy was expecting to receive a further £37. 9s. 9d. It is not clear by what authority Abercorn was collecting this road money: it may have been done by inserting a covenant in the lease.

The 1765 road act introduced a fundamental change in highway adminis-tration.[25] It abolished the six days labour and authorised the grand jury to raise the sums required to build and maintain roads. The procedure was based on the traditional method of raising the county cess to fund bridges and other local government needs such as the court house and gaol belonging to the county. Jemmy explained the major changes to the earl and reckoned that the road-making programme would suffer because the overseer would not be able in future to obtain any money from the county until the grand jury released it on completion of the scheme.

> I can not find that there is any thing substituted by parliament in the room of the parish labour; that money for roads is to be presented by Grand Juries at the assize as formerly, but no money to be paid the overseer till there is an affidavit made before the judge at the assize, that the work is done according to the presentment, and the overseer then

gets from the treasurer whatever he swears he has expended in doing
the work, provided it does not exceed the money presented; I do remember when the overseer got the money the assize after it was presented to
do the work with, the judges finding much money in the county books
not accounted for, ordered the Treasurer to pay no money till he received
an affidavit taken before two justices, that so much was expended
according to the presentment, and then gave their order on the Treasurer
to pay so much, but by this last act there is no account to be made but
before the judge at the assize when the work is finished.

This no doubt will prevent abuses of the public money, yet it is
imagined that the roads will be much neglected as there will not be
many ready to advance money for so long a time, and many think that
if the money when raised was paid to the overseers, and care taken to
make them account in a reasonable time, that the law would have been
better; by the late act the judges have a power to issue executions for
the goods and chattels of the person who has not accounted.[26]

The earl's response was straightforward and practical:

As the roads are put upon a new establishment, I desire you will expend
all the small balance that remains, upon some spot of the public road,
and that you will for the future levy three half pence in the pound rent,
to be expended entirely on private [bye] roads for the use of the
tenants, not to be laid out distinctly within the town[land]s where it is
raised, nor by any means to be worked by the tenants in preference.[27]

Jemmy's forecast that the number and scale of road-making projects would be
reduced, however, proved well wide of the mark because many gentry
provided contractors with loans, believing that their money was safe, and so
the spate of road-building increased. Unfortunately some gentry lost money
in all the excitement.

It was apprehended that the county of Donegal would have been grie-
vously taxed at last assize and the people were in very great commotion
about it and came in crowds to traverse. The tax gatherer of the barony of
Raphoe absconded with upwards of £14,000, and a gentleman's house
was broken the night before the judges came into the county [to hold the
assizes], his desk forced open and upwards of £660 taken off.

The Court was of opinion that the money could not be levied a
second time and that the gentlemen who made the roads have no
redress; the Dean of Raphoe, I am told, was one of those who had
expended upwards of £130.[28]

In 1772 parliament permitted Ulster parishes to impose a parish cess of one penny per acre to maintain minor public roads, or bye-roads, that could not 'without great expense and waste of ground be made of the breadth required' by the 1765 act which had specified a minimum of thirty feet between drains and fences and fourteen feet in breadth for the gravelled road. The right to vote at such vestries was restricted to the better-off Protestant parishioners. Where vestries failed to make presentments or to submit plans to construct or repair roads, parishioners were still to be liable for the traditional six days labour, according to 11 George III c.9. These Ulster parishes retained responsibility for the bye-roads in their districts until it was repealed in 1796 by 35 George III c.55, and passed once more to the grand jury. Such roads were vital to provide access to bogs and transport of lime for the improvement of marginal land, as Jemmy pointed out to the earl:

> I examined the roads to Cavanlee and Edimore mountains; they are convenient enough for the tenants to draw their turf on slide carrs, which and driving their cattle are the only uses they are to them; if people from this place were to bring their turf from thence, a road for wheel carrs, and pulling down a hill or two would be necessary, but I think it would be best that this bog was first all taken.[29]

The construction and maintenance of bridges had long been the responsibility of the grand juries and after the 1765 act they found themselves well-funded to undertake major programmes of bridge building: some of these projects had proved very difficult in the past, notably the bridge between Strabane and Lifford, and continued to give problems:

> Lifford bridge we hope is not in danger, though the arch of that side was thought faulty more than fifteen years ago; it was proposed by those of Donegal to fill it up, but as this county pays equally for that bridge it was objected to in this, as it was thought this town would be more liable to be flooded, yet if it was thought necessary they were ready to join in rebuilding it. There are three arches between this and Lifford: two of them and a great part of the road have been torn away this winter; the road was so bad before last assize, that the county granted £107 to repair it; I am appointed one of the overseers, and I am ready to fall about it; vast sums it has cost since I remember. Mr Barclay who was once an overseer of it, laid out £180, and I believe he had not returned from the assize where he accounted for it, till a flood quite destroyed it; had that happened before the assize he would have lost the money, for the overseer must not only swear that he faithfully expended the money, but that the road is then sufficiently repaired.[30]

Contrary to popular tradition the tenants often played a significant, if not always positive, role in deciding the location and layout of the bye-roads supervised by the estate, as Jemmy reported in a letter to the earl in 1784:

> I was spoken to by some of the tenants of Gortlougher who said Mr Jordan was carrying on a road that was not in the least useful. I fixed with him and we went there yesterday. The road begins at Sian, goes on through the Glentimans into Gortlougher and [is] to go into the great road between Strabane and Magheracreggan at Magheragar. As far as I can judge, it is very [well] laid out through bad grounds, avoiding hills, and a very great convenience to the inhabitants. It really lets out these people that were before shut up. Besides, it goes directly past by the edge of a limestone quarry in Magheragar. It was plain when I went there that the person complaining wanted chiefly to push the road so as to pass by his farm without (I may say) touching him, though the road going as it is intended will (I am persuaded) save his farm and give him a road from his house to the limestone quarry. This very man as it appears was the chief petitioner for the road and said he would be glad to have it though it went straight through his garden.[31]

THE RISE AND FALL OF MAGHERACREGGANN

The townland of Magheracreggan lies on the western boundary of the manor of Derrigoon. Although there is no record of a patent for markets and fairs, *Watson's Almanac* for 1744 notes that fairs were due to be held on Thursday 26 April and Tuesday 13 November. There appears to have been something undisciplined about this community. In 1736 the then agent, Jo. Colhoun, had trouble with its tenants whom he accused of intending

> to bring that market to nothing, as they judge it raised their rents; they do set up standings themselves and those that needs them must pay them more than the ordinary toll. Merchants that set up for themselves, Magheracreggan tenants pulled them down, and say they'll not suffer any cattle to stand on that open street on which the fair stands; they already [im]pounded some, but were forthwith ordered out; they say surveyed and no allowance for the market standing.[32]

This problem does not seem to have been settled at that time because Colhoun reported more than ten years later: 'The tenants of Magheracreggan allege your Lordship laid some rent extraordinary on their town on account of trade and its being a market town.'[33]

In 1751 the earl instructed Colhoun: 'I would have McCrea send me a plan of the new road from my limestone quarry to Magheracreggan, distinguishing the milestones and the houses upon it, and I would also have a plan of the little square at Magheracreggan where the market is kept.'[34]

Although proposals to develop the town were mooted, serious planning did not commence until 1757. Even then Abercorn's advisers differed about the location for the new town. One of them, Michael Priestley of Derry, explained:

> The place Mr Nisbitt thinks most proper in the lands of Magheracreggan for the town is to the north of the present town and near the land of Whitehouse; enclosed your Lordship has the plan for a town divided into lots and adapted to the place; the situation is very agreeable; water is convenient and turf; at some distance there are stones, lime, and sand convenient and I believe clay may be found to make bricks; this is almost at the bounds of your estate and cannot be of the same advantage to you as in another situation, in the improvement of land and all other business; persons living on other lands may follow trade when living near a town with equal advantage to those in the town; this I think a material objection to the fixing the town on the lands of Magheracreggan.
>
> Magheralough is the situation I recommend for the town; here is all the necessaries for building, water and fire convenient and much more agreeable than the other in all respects; the roads will centre here much better than at Magheracreggan and is a shorter line to Drumquin.[35]

Nathaniel Nisbitt, the old agent, had recommended the Magheracreggan site because he thought the earl might have difficulty in obtaining a new patent for markets and fairs in any other townland.[36] The new agent, Jemmy Hamilton, supported the Magheralough recommendation because it had bog in abundance.[37] For some unexplained reason, however, the problem of the site was not settled at this time and the earl set aside his plan to lay out about four thousand feet of front in Magheracreggan. It is possible that he revived the project when he visited the estate in the summer of 1761 but its absence from the correspondence would suggest that it may have been abandoned even before he regained control of Strabane in 1764 and concentrated on its development instead.

In 1772 Jemmy reported that all whiskey stills were to be suppressed in all towns except corporate towns and towns holding weekly markets; he had been so apprehensive for Magheracreggan that he had 'got the people to bring in meal and potatoes every Thursday, and I could do little more than make it nominal.'[38] When he quizzed the collector of the excise he was shown

> several petitions that had been sent to the commissioners by distiller and returned to him to inform them that they must not work. The collector told me that there were some from persons who lived in little market

towns, that he was desired to report the number of houses, and whether suffering them would be for the good of the revenue, by which I would apprehend that they have some latitude by the late act to suppress such if found not for the good of the revenue.[39]

It is unlikely that any concessions were made to Magheracreggan especially in the light of comments made by Jemmy a dozen years later:

The little whiskey houses that are all over the country ruin the people; they are full every market day as they return home and it is in them quarrels are chiefly; if the licence for selling whiskey was made high and encouragement [given] to the ale sellers it might by degrees establish breweries in little towns, or encourage the retailers to brew themselves; I wish they would try in Magheracreggan.[40]

Attempts were made on several occasions to promote the fairs there. Jemmy explained to the earl:

The two old fairs at Magheracreggan are held the 6 May and 24 November. [After the change of the calendar in 1752 the original dates were termed *Old Style* and eleven days added to make them *New Style*] ...They now choose them to be the first Thursday in June, the second in August, the third in October; and fourth in December. We had a very good fair the 18 December just upon its being proclaimed the market before and spread about the people but if our days for the future were fixed, we think of getting some advertisements printed, and to give notice that there will be a cloth market, and as June is a high time for buying, perhaps it may take and continue for the other five days.[41]

Even then the Magheracreggan customs were let for only £5, due to rise to £7 in 1779. In 1788 the inhabitants of Magheracreggan told Jemmy that they had sent a petition to his Lordship because they had very little business as a town and requested that the earl make the fairs and markets there *custom free.* Although the dates of the fairs remained in the almanac, Magheracreggan as a settlement soon disappeared.

MILLS

Water-powered corn mills, known locally as grist-mills, ground oatmeal and malt, and sometimes barley. In Ulster under the plantation scheme a clause in the royal patent by which each estate was granted, had given the landlord the authority to construct a manor mill and to bind his tenants to bring to it for grinding all the grain that they grew on their farms. The group of townlands whose tenants were attached to each mill was known as its *succan*. On the maps of the Abercorn estate completed in 1777, the location of sixteen mills with their associated mill-dams are shown. Traditionally Ulster people have viewed and treated the provision of manor corn mills on an estate either at best as a basic service provided by the landlord for the farming community, or at worst another imposition to increase the income of the landlord: they objected especially to the scale of charges imposed by the miller to whom the landlord had leased the mill.

In leases to these individual tenants the landlord, in a clause known as *suit to mills*, specified the mill each tenant had to attend. The proportion of the grain to be given as payment to the miller for grinding, was measured in bowls of varying sizes ranging from one sixteenth to one fortieth of a sack: this payment was known as the *multure* (pronounced in Ulster as 'mooter'). If there was an under-miller, he was paid as *bannock* one sixty-fourth from each sack. All these three terms, *multure*, *bannock*, and *succan* (or *sucken*), were common to England and Scotland.[42] The lease drew attention also to the financial penalty charged on every bushel of grain that was ground outside the manor: it was generally five shillings a bushel which was reckoned to be much more than the value of the multure.[43] The only way for tenants to evade the payment of multure was to sell the grain in the public market for seed or exchange it for meal.[44]

Whereas in Scotland those tenants who defied their landlord by having their grain ground outside the estate, would have been dealt with by the landowner's officers in his own baronial courts, in Ulster the earl's agents could not prosecute them in his manor courts. Instead, they had to prosecute the defaulters through the civil courts where they were likely to be not only opposed by lawyers but confounded by 'petty juries' composed of tenants from their own and neighbouring estates.[45] Abercorn, therefore, tried not to antagonise tenants and urged his agents to settle disputes quickly and peacefully. After 1758 new leases even permitted tenants to go to any mills on the estate.[46]

It needs to be emphasised that landlords were responsible for both the construction of mills and their restoration at the end of a lease (usually for twenty-one years). By clauses in their leases tenants were required to assist in cleansing and scouring the watercourses for the mills, as directed by the landlord or his agent. The repair of mills, however, was a matter between the landlord and the miller. In return for paying rent to the landlord the millers expected him to compel the tenants to grind at their mills. The whole tone of the correspondence between the earl of Abercorn and his agents does confirm their anxiety for the welfare of the millers whom they encouraged to persevere with promises of support. In the case of Douglas mill, for instance, the tenant, William Sinclair, complained:

Agreeable to your Lordship's commands delivered me by Mr. Hamilton
I have tried Douglas mill another season, I am sorry to say with as little
success as the former; neither is there any reason to hope the toll will
increase, so much of the good ground being occupied with flax and
barley. I can with truth assure your Lordship that on an average the mill
does not make more than fifteen barrels of shilling yearly which comes
greatly short of the rent. I have put entire new works into the mill and
repaired the walls; it yet remains necessary to put a new roof on it and
the water-course by the violence of the late floods is much damaged
which with a millpond which is greatly wanted, will occasion a considerable expense.[47]

In December of that year Jemmy confirmed his fears about Sinclair's plight:

Your Lordship did order me to tell Mr Sinclair who had complained of
his bargain, to go on with his improvements and not to be discouraged,
and upon his second application desired me to make him such an
abatement as an improving tenant deserved, but I find he does not
mean to hold it, and expects to be paid for the money he laid out in
building and otherwise.

Mr Sinclair has laid out much more money [about £200] than he can
bear the loss of, and yet it can never bring your Lordship the fifth of the
value should your Lordship repay him, as things now appear to me.[48]

A few days later Jemmy went to see Mr Sinclair's house and the improvements
at Douglas and reckoned their value at about a third of the £200 Sinclair had
spent. 'The house is placed very conveniently for the farm though it is likely that
a person who would take the mill, would wish to have it on the roadside, as well
for its being near the mill as being a convenient [place] for a shop or a public
house.' Jemmy reckoned that Sinclair would not be in a position to complain 'if
your Lordship lowered the rent so much and left it to him to hold or dispose of
it. Both the corn and flax mills are in very bad order, the walls and timber both
bad: I do not think less than £40 would repair them.'[49] The earl's response was
to lower the rent, backdating it to the commencement of the lease.[50]

Some of the mills gave much more trouble than others, especially those
with an irregular supply of water. Few mills had the capacity to work in a dry
summer while floods on a river could destroy sluices and burst the banks of
the races. It is difficult for us now to appreciate the extent of the damage that
a storm could do then in a comparatively short space of time to the
insubstantial structures that men were able to build with local materials.[51]

The correspondence between Jemmy and the earl provides very valuable
information about the origins of the best known mill in north-west Ulster,
the flour-mill built at Seein (Scian, Sian or Sion) by Galbraith Hamilton in

1760. In 1765 Hamilton petitioned the Irish House of Commons for a grant towards its construction:

> That the lands about the city of Londonderry, Strabane, Lifford, St Johnstown, Raphoe and Castlefinn, are well known to be productive of the best wheat, yet for want of a proper mill for grinding that valuable grain, agriculture hitherto hath been so discouraged there, that the inhabitants were obliged to supply themselves from America by importing flour from thence, which has been attended with very great disadvantages to the kingdom in general, and that part of it in particular; that the Petitioner from these national considerations did, in the year 1760, at a very great expense, erect a wheat mill of the best construction on the great river Mourne within a mile of Strabane, which for its contrivance is, by persons of skill, esteemed equal to any thing of that kind in this kingdom, and so situated as to be supplied with water in the driest seasons. That the Petitioner's mill is situated in the centre of a country where, by its inland navigation from Londonderry to Strabane and Castlefinn, the carriage of wheat is extremely cheap and easy, and from the advantages which have attended the increase of tillage there since erecting said mill, the Petitioner is induced to extend his scheme much further, if encouraged by Parliament, by erecting granaries there and buying up such quantities of wheat as will, at all times enable him to supply that part of the country and prevent large quantities of flour from being imported annually there; that the Petitioner has already expended a very considerable sum on said mill.[52]

In 1779, however, when Galbraith Hamilton was anxious to give up the mill, he told a very different story to his landlord, the earl of Abercorn:

> When I first became the farmer of Sion Mill near fifty years ago, my principal object was thereby to have the command of water for the purpose of erecting a bleachgreen in the adjoining lands, and except in a very dry season I have seldom been able to make your Lordship's rent, the succan of said mill being the tenants of your Lordship's freeholds who in general are bound to mill or mills in the Mourne and could not be brought to grind their grain at Sion Mill, without my entering into obligation with them [i.e. reducing his charges].
>
> About twenty-three years ago Sion Mill being very old and wanted to be rebuilt, I was advised by several persons to add to her a wheat mill which would encourage the cultivation of wheat in this part of the country and to enable me to which your Lordship was pleased to advance me one hundred pounds to be repaid your Lordship by an additional rent of eight pounds a year; and this undertaking cost me above one hundred pounds more, and had the misfortune to find that my expense

of the wheat mill had not the desired effect, and for several years created double expense to me; and being advanced in years and my intention of setting my bleachgreen which I had erected at a great expense to some advantage, was defeated because I could not therewith grant a certainty of the water longer nor I was farmer of Sion Mill.[53]

After Galbraith Hamilton gave up the mill to William Cunningham, the agent persuaded the earl to rebuild the mill to take full advantage of the water power available at this site. By the time it was completed in 1785 by Alexander Stewart it had cost more than £1,000. A considerable proportion of this money had been expended on maximising the supply of water to the mill by blasting and quarrying rock to widen the mill course from four to ten feet: this was to prove of permanent value to this site.[54] In the circumstances both the earl and his agent were anxious to make the mill a success. As well as procuring French millstones for grinding wheat, Jemmy purchased from Belfast a stove to dry malt in a kiln.[55] Finding a miller who could exploit such a mill to repay this substantial investment, would prove more difficult. The agent made little progress with the sitting tenant:

> I have often spoken to Cunningham to make an offer for the mill; his only answer was that he would leave the rent to your Lordship, that he could not judge what it was worth, but that he would give £70 for one year; I told him the unreasonableness of his offer, to advance but £15 when he knew there was upwards of £1,000 laid out now in those works; he repeated his offer, of leaving the rent for this year to your Lordship, and added that his mouterer should keep a book for the key of the mouter chest, and answer on his oath for it, and that his wheat miller should keep an exact account of what he receives for grinding wheat for one year, to which account he would square and this might be a means for settling this year's and the rent in future. The toll he gets is 2s. 8½ d. a barrel and his miller 3d. when he dresses the flour, which taking the average price of wheat from 25s. to 30s. a barrel is from the 9th to the 10th grain. I do think the mill is worth a hundred guineas, and I do think the bleaching green deserves consideration; there are but two greens in this neighbourhood, Mr. Edie's at Burndenet and a Mr Smyly's about 2 miles from this, so that I may say more than four-fifths of our brown linen goes near thirty miles to be bleached; the carriage, I dare say, is 3d a web: beside, the owner of the cloth would think it a great matter to have his cloth so near him that he could go and see how it went on without much trouble.[56]

It is ironic that farmers were prepared to pay a toll in cash for the grinding and preparation of their wheat, equal to between one-ninth and one-tenth of its value when they had previously fought to drive down the toll on grinding oatmeal from one-sixteenth to one-twentieth or even one-thirtieth. Jemmy's suggestion about the construction was farsighted because the following two decades were to witness a considerable expansion in the output of linen webs of an improved quality in the Foyle basin: the bleaching and finishing of webs purchased from the weavers in the markets of Strabane, Omagh and Newtownstewart brought prosperity to the bleachgreens near Limavady and Coleraine.

On 9 June 1785 James Hamilton reported to the earl in London about a visit he had paid to Seein mill:

> The want of water at other mills had brought great numbers there with their grain; there were some from Drumcrow and from Lignatraw, and from places at a greater distance. Both mills were grinding oaten meal. How soon and how well the business was done, I observed it to Cunningham; he said nothing could do better than the mills and that if they were to have such business as they then had, they would be worth a vast deal, but said nothing about advancing the rent. I then told him that your Lordship had ordered me to have land laid off to the mill [for the mill-farm], from about twenty to twenty-five acres.[57]

Because Cunningham continued to evade all discussions about a lease that would bring a more realistic return for the expenditure on the mill, the agent was compelled to look for another tenant. On 17 November when he reported to Abercorn his initial impressions of the new miller, he may have begun to realise how difficult it would be for the new mill to earn a considerable rent:

> William Patterson is I believe a cheerful honest man and will make a faithful return of the produce of the mills, yet the value of them can not be ascertained by that. As yet we grow but little wheat, so that what is paid for grinding it and dressing the flour, must turn out but to little account. The man who would take these mills ought, I am told, to have £1,000 at least employed in that business. Cunningham, I suppose had about £200 this year in that business and I dare say made much more of it, than by what came in to be ground for payment.[58]

In his reply the earl instructed Hamilton to let the mill to Patterson for £112. He also offered to lend the new tenant £300 interest free, provided that £100 of the principal would be paid off punctually each year.

The Seein mill project was very ambitious and its financial success depended on the ability of farmers in the Foyle valley to produce regular crops of wheat that would compete in price with that imported from America. The local climate, however, was not warm enough to ripen the wheat thoroughly every year. It was unlikely also that a sufficient demand for wheaten flour could be generated in the Foyle basin to make financial investment profitable. Another century would pass before the great flax-spinning mill with water-powered turbines at Sion Mills would justify the confidence of Jemmy Hamilton and his master, the earl of Abercorn, in developing the site.

The study of this correspondence about the mills exposes significant changes occurring in the rural economy. The agent had become convinced of the potential of this industrial site on the estate and had persuaded the landlord to invest a considerable sum in its development. The earl was playing a strong supportive role in the development of an entrepreneurial culture on his estates by providing capital and writing off bad debts. The agent, Jemmy Hamilton, kept the landlord well-informed about the minutiae and the context of the progress of major projects so that problems were not allowed to run out of control. Neither landlord nor agent made the mistake of trying to engage directly in the business themselves, as many landlords had done to their cost.

MINING

On at least two occasions during the administration of the eighth earl, professionals were hired to search for minerals at locations believed to be worth examination. In April 1758 the earl sent two Scottish colliers, Angus Beaton and Alexander Taylor, to tour the manor of Magavelin in Donegal and they were required to send him weekly reports of their progress. As they had no success at any of the locations, they were recalled in October: the whole operation had cost almost £40.[59]

Ten years later two Scottish leadminers arrived to carry out a search for lead. Jemmy Hamilton reported to the earl: ' No people I think ever wrought more constant than the miners do and the labourer I may say never ceases striking the jumper that they bore with; the expense of sharpening the tools is very much; they have 18 jumpers and they have been all sharpened twice in one day.'[60] They too reported regularly to the earl. They had no more success than the colliers although they stayed a year. On their return journey, however, one of them died suddenly in Antrim. Both expeditions did have postscripts:

> Knox who carries on the potter's business near Derry sent up a person to see the lead ore and to inquire the price as it was wanted for glazing earthenware; the man saw it and liked it very well but said it was not saleable till it was cleanly picked and washed; in that state he said it would be worth some £10 to £12; the miner says that we have fully a ton; if your Lordship approves of its being sold, the miner advises I should send for Carr, the miner that left us to prepare it.[61]

There is no evidence to suggest that this offer was taken up by the earl. The other news was that a flood on the River Mourne had torn away part of the bank of a tributary, the Sian brook, and discovered coal about 32 feet below the surface and 400 yards from the River Mourne.[62] Abercorn commented: 'The coal at Sian affords some prospect for posterity against the time when the bogs are worn out.'[63]

BRICKMAKING

The development of towns and villages in the Foyle valley had stimulated other local industries, notably brickmaking. A tenant who found a deposit of suitable clay on his farm, was inclined to experiment before he sought the permission of his landlord and so it was up to the agent to carry out regular inspections. In 1751, for example, Jo. Colhoun reported to the earl:

> I have viewed three brickyards in Donelong manor, vizt James Paterson at the ferry boat who says he had made bricks seven years past and alleges he had leave; his clay pits are close on his mearing with Menagh Hill and surely does some damage, but he has smoothed the surplus pretty well and it will be good pasture; says he also depends more on the bricks than on the ferry for his rent as he has great loss by several persons on both sides of the river having small boats who ferry over passengers without any exception and some take money on public days.[64]

Although the agent was ready to turn a blind eye to such depredations, the earl made it clear to his chief agent, Nathaniel Nisbitt, that he intended to control them.[65] By 1770, however, John Hamilton reported: 'There are so many brickyards already between this town and Derry that the owners cannot get their bricks sold; Luke of Ballydonnaghy hath many thousands unsold'.[66]

John's brother, James, reckoned that brick refuse had proved an ideal dressing for certain kinds of land:

> I do think the brickyards are beneficial to the estate for the land that the clay is dug from if properly levelled and dressed, may in general be bettered, and good rents arise from them at present. The refuse of brick of which there must be a good deal wherever they burn, is the best thing I know for improving sour grass, which generally grows on those cold bottoms where brick clay is found. I have recommended it to them and I know Thomas Patton has tried it with success. I cannot say anything about the rest but I do propose to see them and try to persuade them to do it. I think clay well burned is preferable to lime for such land.[67]

LIMEKILNS

Limestone had been used to fertilise land in Ulster since the plantation and the Abercorn estate was well supplied. It is surprising, therefore, that this estate was so slow to follow the lead of the eastern counties where Arthur Young in 1776 praised farmers for their skill in applying 'burned lime' to newly-broken land, especially turf-bog.[68] As early as 1770 Jemmy had drawn the attention of the earl to a Mr Fairly who 'carries on the salt and lime business in Derry; the fuel that boils his salt, burns his limestone, so that he can afford the lime almost for half of what it can be got for elsewhere; we are often supplied in this town with lime from him.'[69]

In January 1788, however, Jemmy told the earl, 'I find lime kilns are much desired, if they could be fixed on some good plan' and added that he had asked one of the tenants to inspect a kiln installed in a limestone quarry on a neighbouring Donegal estate. A month or so later he reported that a local mason had furnished a design that convinced him.

> The objections to the large one is their not being able on account of the turf smoke to supply the kiln with limestone and turf which should be laid down regularly in layers. The little kilns before they are fired could be properly filled or set fire to and someone drawing the lime, another burning and the third filling.

He reckoned that a kiln should be managed like a mill: 'a substantial tenant who could hire men to raise stone and get turf etc., would carry on the business best.'[70] By November of the same year eight kilns had been built at strategic places throughout the several manors at an average cost of about £45 each, and 8,600 loads of turf cut to supply them with fuel. Jemmy visited two of them to see them filled and burning. He reassured the earl that the whole project was being executed in a businesslike manner:

> We measured the limestone and turf put into each kiln and keep a very particular account of every expense so as to be able to ascertain the price for the lime. I suppose for a year or two they will turn out to little account, yet I think in some time it will make a great change in the estate. The people in general have some little limestone raised that they will burn and perhaps raise more before they buy, but as some will use it and show plainly the great good of it, the rest will either raise more themselves or buy, either of which will improve the estate.[71]

LINEN INDUSTRY

An address from the inhabitants of Strabane to the earl of Abercorn soon after he regained control of that borough in 1765, recalled 'Your noble ancestors set up, supported and established ours, without a rival in trade, and they gave birth and maturity to the linen manufacture our staple commodity, now falling into a languishing state'.[72] This compliment struck a favourable note for the earl was proud of his family's record in promoting the industry.[73] There is evidence of a linen demonstration and competition in Strabane in 1700 when local people were awarded prizes for their skill. and in 1708 Thomas Molyneux when passing through Strabane, noted that the town belonged to Lord Abercorn 'who has here something of the linen manufacture.'[74] This was the sixth earl (1701–34) who claimed a year before his death that he had 'at my own great expense promoted the linen industry in that neighbourhood ... which has so far succeeded that at Strabane is now the greatest staple of linen yarn in the kingdom'.[75]

The eighth earl and his agents were not involved in the industry except for submitting applications to the Linen Board for grants of spinning wheels and click-reels that they could then distribute among their tenants. In 1753, for example, Nathaniel Nisbitt informed the earl: 'Your Lordship has got many blessings in Strabane for the wheels, and indeed this season is much harder on the little people who live in towns than those who live in the country; provisions of all sorts being higher than ever I knew them, this time of the year.[76] Later in the same year Nisbitt reported: 'The Linen Board has granted to your Lordship's estates for the present year 50 wheels and 10 reels; what will your Lordship be pleased to order about them?'[77] Two months later he had to remind him: 'Will your Lordship be pleased to direct me how I shall dispose of the wheels, whether your Lordship would have them spun for, or divided amongst the poorer sort of tenants.[78] These references confirm that the preparation of flax, the spinning of yarn and its reeling into standard hanks for sale to the weavers, were providing employment, especially in the town of Strabane. The situation of the poorer classes did not improve significantly throughout the 1750s. Jemmy Hamilton reported in 1759:

> The people that are backward were, as I understand, much in debt as well for their rents and tithes as for their subsistence in our late hard times, to discharge which they got money advanced, mostly by yarn buyers, to whom they were obliged to give their yarn, as they spun it, at much an undervalue, nor durst they dispute any price offered them by the lenders, as that would destroy their credit with them. This I hope, if our markets hold, will soon be over and the people will have it in their power to sell to the best advantage.[79]

There were high hopes for the success of the linen industry on the estate when in 1750 Jo. Colhoun, the Strabane agent, reported: 'They are about to build a new market-house in Strabane early next spring with a linen hall and vaults and have got £400 subscribed for towards the building.'[80] The project, however, staggered on until the earl regained control of the corporation in 1764 and injected fresh impetus into the scheme. The initial proposal to have facilities in the market-house for linendrapers must have failed because in 1770 another proposal was made to construct sheds that would be divided by a brick wall down the centre to separate the butchers' shambles on one side from the linendrapers on the other.[81]

In 1770 Jemmy was able to tell the earl that his kinsman, William Brownlow of Lurgan, who represented County Armagh in parliament and was an active member of the Linen Board, had proved a good friend to the industry in Strabane:

> Mr Brownlow wrote me that he had found that there had been 60 wheels ordered your Lordship's tenants in the year 1766 which must be forfeited if an affidavit was not sent to the Linen Board that they had been bespoke before last February; he let me know that there were 60 more granted last Board; he says that 5s a wheel is what is allowed, and he advises that good wheels should be got made here, and the people who get, to pay the difference; he has I believe procured John Lowry of Drumcrow some considerable encouragement for carrying on the bleaching business, and got the brown scals for another of your Lordship's tenants.[82]

There were other interesting developments although the outbreak of the American War of Independence in 1775 postponed many of them:

> I find there was last spring and summer a great quantity of tow spun into coarse yarn which was chiefly woven into yard wides, and was sold for soldiers' shirts and for sheets, so that there was a less quantity of Coleraines [the official name for linens 7/8th yard wide] made; that and, as we suppose, the expectation of an agreement with the American colonies, where a large quantity of our linens of various kinds, both printed and plain, were vended well, occasioned very brisk dealing, and the good sale the bleachers had in Dublin and London in June and July made them go on very briskly till the September market came on in Dublin when it appeared that the keenness for buying had very much abated, as large quantities of goods of the former market remained unsold, and I know a great many whose cloth lies in their factor's hands, and have been prevented for want of money, and others who could buy but will not venture, as they are not encouraged by their friends in London and Dublin.[83]

When Edward Willes as chief baron of the Exchequer came to hold the assizes in Londonderry in 1762 he commented: 'Though they make a great deal of linen cloth about Derry yet they do not work up into cloth so much as they might do but principally supply Manchester with linen yarn which is exported to Liverpool; and a Manchester factor is one of the best trades in Derry.'[84] Derry's exports of linen yarn to England reached more than 17,000 cwt in 1783 but declined to just under 4,000 by 1792 and rarely exceeded 2,000 after 1803.[85] This was due to a series of English inventions in cotton spinning that produced strong warp threads, thus greatly reducing the demand for Irish linen warps. The availability of more local yarn, however, encouraged many people in north-west Ulster to take up weaving and their output was reflected in the rapid expansion of the linen markets of Derry, Strabane, and Newtownstewart.[86]

TURBARY

Turbary is defined in law as the right to go on to another person's land and to dig and take away turf for use as fuel. In the early decades of the plantation scheme landlords allocated to each of their tenants, by a clause in their leases, the right to take a fixed amount of turf annually from a named bog. To prevent turbary from generating quarrels between tenants, especially over trespass, it was essential to place it under the supervision of an estate moss-bailiff. In 1764 Jemmy as agent was certainly both relieved and pleased to welcome the appointment of one on the Abercorn estate and noted how the duties of this role might be extended towards the reclamation of bogs:

> I really believe the institution of Kelsey may in great measure answer your Lordship's expectations. Before he was appointed, there was for the whole turf-cutting season constant complaints among the tenants which, though sometimes but trivial, could not be so properly determined by any of your Lordship's agents as by him. Last year he laid (I believe) through all your Lordship's estates in these parts, each person's proportion of bog with directions how they should manage it. He assured me he would see whether they had observed them and make alterations where he found it necessary; that he would mark down any place where there was more than sufficient bog to supply the adjacent tenants and if reclaimable, direct how it should be done; and where from its situation it was valuable as turf, inform the agent of it and its value. He measured and rated the hill of wood enclosed in Widow Brady's land in Drumlegagh. He has laid off passes between the holdings in Envagh and in many places to bogs. I am sure he might be very well employed in laying out drains in this great bog and cutting out lots for setting, and though at present as the turf are bad they could not set for much, yet

certainly if they had some time of them and managed it properly, not only the bog would be improved, but the skirtings near the land.[87]

By the mid-eighteenth century it was evident that resources of peat were under pressure in those areas where turf was expended, population dense, or linen-bleaching concentrated. Its cost depended also on the distance it was carried. Where turf-cutting was an industry cost calculations were made by the *hundred*. After turf was cut, castled and dried in the bog it was built into clamps eight feet long, four feet high, and six feet wide, 'tapering to the top like the roof of a house'. Twenty clamps comprised a hundred. By 1800 a hundred of turf was transported in forty wheel-cars or one hundred and twenty slide-cars (an indication that a wheel-car could transport three times as much as a slide-car). It was reckoned that a hundred could be won for £1. 16s. of which 15s. went for drawing and 14s. for cutting, and would fetch from £2. 3s. 4d. in summer to £5. 8s. 4d. in winter. The cost of working a bog depended on its distance from a market town and its condition. Where the bog was well-drained and firm the turf could be cut easily with a spade and castled nearby but if it was too soft the bog had to be cut 'abreast and overhand' which made it more expensive:

> I find that it [Ballyfatten bog, the only one near this town] is set in leases from £2 to £4 per acre according to its distance and goodness but that £3 is the general price. And as it is made bog they can have 800 loads on each acre and those cut and saved at 10s. per hundred, whereas your Lordship's bog being yet soft and the turf requiring to be laid out at a greater distance the acre would scarcely contain 600 loads nor will it stand the spade but must be cut abreast and overhand which makes the price 15s. for cutting and saving. Besides the received computation is that 200 of Ballyfatten turf are equal to 300 of low bog but that they may draw 3 from this for 2 from Ballyfatten.[88]
>
> The price of carriage is in proportion to the number of turns from each bog, and the general computation by the hundred of turf is thought to be 10s. 10d. from your Lordship's bog and 16s. 3d. from Ballyfatten.[89]

By the mid eighteenth century bogland was acquiring a commercial value, especially when it was drained by ditches and opened up by access roads. John Hamilton in Strabane recommended 'Forty shillings an acre will be a sufficient rent and as the roads will sometimes want repair, if your Lordship thinks it proper, to fix two days work of man and horse yearly on every acre, I would hope that would keep them in order.'[90]

The earl would have preferred to set the bogs not to individuals but to tenants prepared to take responsibility for organising their subletting. Jemmy explained that the culture of the local tenants precluded such a move:

I have heard your Lordship say that you would be better pleased to set a number of acres of turf to one who would make it a business to take care of it, than setting single acres. I am sure it would be best though none would undertake to cut, save, and sell the turf. Yet if the tenant of the land would take a number of acres, and even set them off to others, the tenant no doubt would take care of the management of the bog, but none of them will offer to take till he finds it will be taken by others.

Forty shillings an acre was thought a sufficient price for Galdanaugh bog but I am pretty sure it would just now set at £3 an acre and if Barclay had the setting of it, perhaps more.[91]

An aspect of turbary that is often overlooked was the reclamation of timber from the bogs. In 1802 John McEvoy in his *Statistical survey of the county of Tyrone* recorded: 'The chief reliance the county has, is upon bog-fir, which many of the bogs produce in great plenty, but it is in general attended with great difficulty and expence in being able to manage it, for want of roads, and proper conveniencies to raise it.'[92] Raising bog-timber had long been practised on the Abercorn estate and demand was becoming so strong that the agent needed the landlord to regularize the practice:

Many apply for permits and I am at a loss how to act as some raise and dispose of the timber ... When I find they are about to build I allow them, they filling up the holes and engaging to show any stick they may get to the woodranger or the bailiff, and if fit for that purpose I will pay for their trouble in raising it. There are many applications for raising and drawing away limestone. It is often a damage to the persons through whose lands it is drawn, and they sometimes point out a way it may be drawn and avoid hurting them. If I find the inconvenience in drawing much more than the damage done and the the person is willing to pay what trespass two neighbours may think fit, I direct that they may have liberty; the same in drawing turf. Your Lordship's former determination relative to divisions to be made by the tenants in their farms, has prevented many disputes as to that, and if your Lordship would please to direct something as to permits for raising timber, and trespass for lime and turf drawing, I am sure it would effectually settle them also.[93]

CULTIVATION AND PRESERVATION OF TREES

In theory the landlord owned all the timber on an estate and so he was the only person who could give permission for it to be cut down. Even if a tenant planted trees on his farm, he could not cut down any of them until the expiration of the lease: an act of 1721 allowed him to take a third of them and a 1731 act raised this proportion to one half. An act of 1765 permitted a tenant at the expiration of his lease to claim the trees he had planted, or their value, provided he had lodged a certificate of the trees planted with the clerk of the peace for the county.

Although trees were often planted in the new hedgerows, those that were required for commercial purposes were grown in plantations defined and surrounded by a wall or a fence. There they were regularly thinned by the wood-ranger while tanners paid to strip the bark off oak trees that would then be sold for their timber. The agent Jo. Colhoun, for example, told the earl: 'Thomas Allan has given me in sixty-one sacks of bark sold at £47. 10s. and from 10 to 15 sacks yet unsold. Twelve score pounds make a sack and one sack to the score of sacks is the custom with tanners.'[94] Several letters in the correspondence provide details about work in these plantings:

> On Monday the 30th of last month [May] we began to cut Sooley, the timber as yet but indifferent; there are some pretty well-grown oaks and many small ones drawn up very high by being so very much choked up; we have touched no oak though in some places ther are five or six young plants growing out of one stool; I think it's better they should remain so, till now that they are opened about, they recover some strength, for some of the tall weak ones that stand by themselves will, I fear, be blown down; there are but two cutting and nine other labourers caning and cleaning away the rubbish and John Hyndman who oversees them; the people don't come to buy; as yet they are busy with the turf, and till the sale becomes brisk, I will not employ more labourers.[95]

Much timber and bark was stolen from these woods despite the presence of resident wood-rangers, some of whom were not above suspicion of cutting or selling for their personal profit. The problem of guarding these woods against even their guardians was well-explained by John Sinclair of Hollyhill, another of Abercorn's agents, after he investigated rumours brought to his attention:

> The latter end of August Mr George Hamilton told me he believed the wood at Menaghhill was destroying . . . In two days I went to Joseph Osburn, the wood keeper; he told me there was no oak cut, that a man living above Donemana brought some green oak wattles to make his tent at the fair but that they were not cut at Menaghhill, that there had been some ash cut long before this time, but that for six months past there was none cut except two ash and two alder trees that had been cut with saws on a Sunday night, that he hoped he would find out who cut them as he had got some intelligence, but as yet he has made no discovery.
>
> Some time later I applied to Mr Pearson to view the wood as he formerly cut some alder in it; he sent me the enclosed [letter] which

though very disagreeable to your Lordship I take the liberty to send; indeed from what judgement I could make when I went to see the wood, I believe it is truth, and that all the ash is cut that was worth cutting, though Joseph Osburn never told me; I really believe a wood will not be preserved there as I suspect your Lordship's tenants to be the principal destroyers of it, and they will not discover upon each other though several of them and others have been examined upon oath. There is scarce one acre of that wood yet stubbed or cleaned by James Cunningham or Joseph Osburn since their renting it, which is an excuse for people going into it for rods or wattles.[96]

The law permitted officials of the estate to enter property in search of stolen timber and bark. In July 1769 a party found in the barn of James Baird of Upper Creaghcor

a vessel with eighteen calf skins and three stirk [bullock] skins all in bark ouse, but no bark in layers between them as is commonly used; he showed a receipt for 92 lbs of bark bought from Mr Bond at the water side dated that day as it was sent for after the leather was found for that quantity now and formerly delivered; from the very exorbitant price of leather I'm told it is common for men to buy a small quantity of bark and procure more as they best can for private tannage; these twenty-one skins could not all be for family's consumption though very numerous.[97]

In his reply to the agent, John Sinclair, the earl pointed out: 'There does not seem to be evidence tending to the conviction of anybody of stripping the oaks. But you will do well to have the parties punished upon the foot of tanning privately. It is a great nuisance, and whether it is for sale, or for private consumption is immaterial.'[98] Private tanning was illegal under an act of 10 William III c. 12 because the premises gave off such a foul smell. Several months passed before Sinclair brought an end to the affair and informed the earl:

In observance to your Lordship's last letter, I sent for James Baird, David Kerr, and John Leech, the three private tanners; they chose to refer themselves to the two Mr Hamiltons [Jemmy and John, the Abercorn agents] rather than go to the quarter sessions; they did not deny the fact; James Baird produced Mr Bond's receipt for payment for 83 lb. of bark; swore he never bought bark suspected to be stolen nor did he ever steal or use bark privately obtained; he was fined 20s; David Kerr produced witness to the buying of his bark and after his manner of swearing with uplifted hand declared he never used stolen bark but always, but always, bought bark honestly; he was fined 15s; John Leech for one slink [i.e. premature] calf skin I believe did the same and was fined 5s.[99]

It is interesting, but not surprising, that the three men who could not deny private tanning, preferred to pay a fine that would go to the poor of the parish rather than take their punishment at the quarter sessions. A similar punishment was suggested for tenants or others guilty of taking wood from any of the plantings on the estate:

> Very often grand juries ignore the bills for cutting sticks when the value sworn to is small. Perhaps if your Lordship imposed a fine in proportion to the value found, perhaps four times the value, they would I dare say pay it and it would be a sort of a punishment and a reward to the wood-rangers . . . Andrew Rogers of Broadlea, who is a very good improving tenant, showed me some fences he had made, on which he had planted osiers which he used to sell every third year for about £6. He says they used to steal some of them every year but this last year they mauled them greatly.[100]

While timber was in growing demand on the estate in the closing decades of the eighteenth century, stealing it had become such a serious problem that tenants did not heed the exhortations to plant trees. The estate, therefore decided to follow the example of planting on a commercial scale set on the neighbouring Blessington estate under the supervision of John McEvoy, the author of the *Statistical survey of the county of Tyrone*. It contains an excellent report by him on the planting of the Blessington estate while this Abercorn correspondence contains considerable information about his activities around Baronscourt including a letter from him to the new marquess in 1790.[101]

All of the topics examined in this chapter are worth studying in detail because they provide us with a deeper understanding of the fundamental problems that faced the members of this society in their struggle to maintain their families and improve their future prospects. The reclamation of land, the winning of turf for fuel and bog timber for building, the construction and maintenance of mills, and the construction of the Strabane canal, all reflect their struggle to harness the forces of nature to tame the environment. We can begin, too, to appreciate how the estate and other local institutions tried to organise projects for the welfare of the community and how this interfered with the independence and initiatives of individuals in pursuit of their own goals.

Conclusion

Anyone who reads through the Abercorn estate correspondence will be struck by its value for the study of rural life in eighteenth century Ireland. It is much more immediate and valuable than the often superficial observations of travellers and gives deeper insight into the mentalities and cultures of once living communities. Further study makes the reader aware of themes that pulse through it and emanate their own specific characteristics. It is important to try to identify those themes, to consider their origins, their development, and their significance, local, regional, or national, long term or short term, positive or negative.

The most common theme is the continual subdivision of townlands into ever smaller, compact and enclosed farms to be held under lease from the landlord by individual families. While Abercorn permitted the sale of leases, he insisted that both the old and new tenants should recognise the authority of the estate office and that each party should pay a year's rent for permission. He was prepared also to renew leases to good tenants at the fall of an original lease but he acquired also a reputation for creating new tenants on occasion by leasing to sub-tenants those portions of farms that they had occupied under the previous leaseholder. He maintained this policy which increased the number of lease-holders, in spite of his knowledge that the general trend in Scotland was to create larger and more profitable farms by terminating subtenancies and even tenancies. The argument that in Ireland landlords granted leases for lives in order to create voters at parliamentary elections, does not apply here because it is well-known that the eighth earl was not active in Irish elections while the leases that he granted were not for lives (essential to create a freeholder qualified to vote in an election) but for years. At the same time it should be acknowledged that Abercorn's leasing policy treated honest tenants with due respect.

Abercorn, however, was also a strict disciplinarian. He paid no heed to arguments in favour of granting leases for three lives and even reduced the length of leases from twenty-one years to seven years in order to put pressure on those tenants who would not execute the covenants agreed in the leases. His policy of creating tenants out of former undertenants forced leaseholders to protect themselves against the ambitions of under-tenants by admitting them only as cottiers without any legal rights whatever. Although Abercorn's principles seem to have been personal, they appear to have been accepted by the tenantry because they were applied fairly and recognised the rights that tenants thought they possessed. On the fall of a lease Abercorn was prepared to grant a renewal to any tenant who had behaved well during his lease. His policy may have differed in detail but not fundamentally from those that governed landlord-tenant relations on other Ulster estates.

Abercorn's policy in the long run had a powerful impact on the physical landscape of the estate. On many estates distinctive clusters of buildings had grown around a convenient spot near the centre of each townland: the spread of leases led to a gradual dispersal of the clusters as new families erected cottages and out-buildings on their own farms. The estate maps that determined or confirmed these changes are bound up in a great book of some ninety-one maps prepared in 1777 for the Tyrone manors and in 1781 for the Donegal manors.[1] To measure the rate of change these maps require to be compared with another set for the same townlands made in 1806 by Henry Hood and David Leslie, as well as an earlier set in 1756.

It could be argued that Abercorn's leasing policy was designed to encourage tenants to bring goods to market for sale. Abercorn's agents attended local markets and fairs to supervise their administration and ensure fair treatment for all those who attended. Abercorn insisted that his agents should keep him informed about market prices, especially for the two major commodities, linen yarn and oatmeal, the staple food. It was the ever-growing demand for these two commodities that compelled landlords to take an active role in the parish vestries in order to promote the construction of roads. There is clear evidence that Abercorn was raising road money from his tenants, either through the parish vestry system or with the rent. The expansion of the road network played a major role in altering the appearance of the landscape by bringing more marginal land into regular occupation and encouraging tenants to link their holdings to the most convenient roads. These developments also are illustrated on the estate maps. The 1765 Road Act ensured that the maintenance and construction of the roads would become a regular charge on the county cess, or rates, so providing a major new source of employment. The improvement of the roads was itself reflected in the development of vehicles and in the increasing range of services provided for travellers, such as post-chaises and stage-coaches.

Whether landlords realised it or not, they had become engaged also in a campaign to rationalise local government and politics through the grand jury and to organise or adapt local bodies to execute decisions that they had agreed in the House of Commons in Dublin. Because municipal corporations had been emasculated to protect the political property of their owners, it was necessary to select local townspeople to serve on market juries and enforce trading standards. The first half of George III's reign contained several other acts that revived traditional local government institutions such as parish vestries and manor courts and extended their responsibilities to institute county hospitals and houses of industry, to provide fire engines, and to settle small claims and debts.[2]

To what extent did the landlord class play an influential role in the economic and social development of Ireland in the eighteenth century? Their contribution needs still to be examined in detail. Malcomson has argued that the Abercorns 'remained the patrons [of Strabane] in that they were the ground landlord, town-planner, promoter of trade and industry and source of what social security there was there.'[3] This essay has demonstrated that although he was an absentee, the eighth earl of Abercorn played a key role in the management and development of this estate. A thorough reappraisal of the role of the estates will have to be undertaken before the history of eighteenth century Ireland can be written.

Notes

This essay is based mainly on the correspondence from the collection of the Abercorn estate papers held in the Public Record Office of Northern Ireland as D/623.

INTRODUCTION

1 Edward Wakefield, *An account of Ireland, statistical and political*, (2 vols, Dublin, 1812), i, p.244.
2 For a detailed introduction to the Abercorn collection by Dr A. P.W. Malcomson see the PRONI website (*proni.nics.gov.uk*) under 'Collections'.
3 J. H. Gebbie (ed.), *An introduction to the Abercorn letters* (Omagh, 1972).
4 Anthony Malcomson, 'The politics of "natural right": the Abercorn family and Strabane borough' in G. A. Hayes-McCoy (ed.), *Historical Studies X* (Clo Chois Fharraige, 1976), pp 43–90.
5 Martin Dowling, *Tenant right and agrarian society in Ulster* (Dublin, 1999); John Dooher, chapters 5, 6, and 8 in *The fair river valley: Strabane through the ages* (Belfast, 2000) edited by John Dooher and Michael Kennedy.
6 W. A. Maguire, *The Downshire estates in Ireland 1801–1845* (Oxford, 1972).
7 James Kelly (ed.), *The letters of Lord Chief Baron Edward Willes to the earl of Warwick 1757–62* (Aberystwyth, 1990), p. 96.

LANDLORD AND AGENTS

1 William Roulston, 'The evolution of the Abercorn estate in north west Ulster, 1610–1703' in *Familia* xv (1999), pp 54–67.
2 Introduction to Abercorn collection on PRONI website. I wish to thank Michael Cox of Gullane in East Lothian for clarifying some details about the Abercorn estates at Dudingston and Paisley respectively.
3 John Gamble, *A view of society and manners in the north of Ireland* (London, 1813), quoted in Gebbie, *Abercorn Letters*, p. ix.

4 Abercorn to Rev. Dr Pelissier, 1 August 1753 (D/623/A/14/84).
5 Malcomson, 'Politics of "Natural Right"', p. 58.
6 Nathaniel Nisbitt to Abercorn, 24 January 1744 (D/623/A/27/5).
7 N. Nisbitt to Abercorn, 19 April 1757 (D/623/A/32/67).
8 J. Colhoun to Abercorn, 16 May 1747 (D/623/A/28/47).
9 *Nomine poenae* was the legal term used for the extra charge that a landlord or his agent could impose when the rent was 21 days overdue, usually a shilling in the £ or 5 per cent.
10 N. Nisbitt to Abercorn, 20 May 1757 (D/623/A/32/74).
11 N. Nisbitt to Abercorn, 9 May 1755, (D/623/A/31/84).
12 N. Nisbitt to Abercorn, 19 April 1757 (D/623/A/32/67).
13 N. Nisbitt to Abercorn, 15 December 1757 (D/623/A/32/96).
14 Joshua Nisbitt to Abercorn, 4 January 1765, (D/623/A/36/95).
15 N. Nisbitt to Abercorn, 15 May 1759 (D/623/A/33/89).
16 James Hamilton to Abercorn, 13 February 1767 (D/623/A/37/59).
17 James Pearson to Abercorn, 16 October 1759 (D/623/A/33/119).
18 Abercorn to John Hamilton, 17 December 1765 (D/623/A/18/44).
19 John Hamilton to Abercorn, 12 January 1766 (D/623/A/37/3).
20 Abercorn to John Hamilton, 24 January 1766 (D/623/A/18/49).
21 James Jordan to Abercorn, 26 December 1779 (D/623/A/43/264).
22 Conn O'Donnell to Abercorn, 28 December 1779 (D/623/A/43/266).

LANDLORD AND TENANTS

1 See W. H. Crawford, 'The significance of landed estates in Ulster, 1600–1820' in *Irish Economic & Social History* xvii (1990), pp 44–61.

2 N. Nisbitt to Abercorn, 24 February 1749 (D/623/A/29/45).

3 N. Nisbitt to Abercorn, 19 April 1757 (D/623/A/32/67).

4 Abercorn to James Hamilton, 25 July 1773 (D/623/A/21/44).

5 James Hamilton to Abercorn, 13 August 1773 (D/623/A/40/108).

6 Abercorn to James Hamilton, 2 September 1773 (D/623/A/21/51).

7 Abercorn to John Hamilton, 12 April 1774 (D/623/A/21/87).

8 James Hamilton to Abercorn, 30 May 1767 (D/623/A/37/75).

9 Abercorn to James Hamilton, 2 November 1769 (D/623/A/19/105).

10 James Hamilton to Abercorn, 12 November 1769 (D/623/A/38/172).

11 James Hamilton to Abercorn, 28 May 1771, (D/623/A/39/122).

12 James Hamilton to Abercorn, 2 June 1771 (D/623/A/39/124).

13 James Hamilton to Abercorn, 6 August 1780 (D/623/A/44/43).

14 James Hamilton to Abercorn, 21 January 1780 (D/623/A/44/6).

15 James Hamilton to Abercorn, 25 January 1780 (D/623/A/44/8).

16 James Hamilton to Abercorn, 22 April 1781 (D/623/A/44/85).

17 James Hamilton to Abercorn, 29 April 1781 (D/623/A/44/87).

18 James Hamilton to Abercorn, 25 April 1773 (D/623/A/40/90).

19 J. McClintock to Abercorn, 13 June 1745 (D/623/A/12/52).

20 N. Nisbitt to Abercorn, 26 June 1753 (D/623/A/30/182); see also 12 August 1753 (D/623/A/30/186).

21 Abercorn to N. Nisbitt, 20 July 1753 (D/623/A/14/83).

22 Abercorn to John Sinclair, 4 October 1769 (D/623/A/19/102).

23 James Hamilton to Abercorn, 14 January 1770 (D/623/A/39/4).

24 James Hamilton to Abercorn, 27 January 1771 (D/623/A/39/101).

25 Abercorn to James Hamilton, 1 January 1771 (D/623/A/20/46) and 7 February 1771 (D/623/A/20/54).

26 James Hamilton to Abercorn, 17 February 1771 (D/623/A/39/104).

27 James Hamilton to Abercorn, 2 August 1771 (D/623/A/39/135).

28 James Hamilton to Abercorn, 17 April 1772 (D/623/A/40/25).

29 James Hamilton to Abercorn, 4 August 1772 (D/623/A/40/55).

30 James Hamilton to Abercorn, 29 February 1788 (D/623/A/47/56).

31 James Hamilton to Abercorn, 16 January 1789 (D/623/A/47/78).

32 Montaigne, *Essais* (M. Rat's edition 1958), I.xxxix.

33 James Hamilton to Abercorn, 9 July 1784 (D/623/A/45/32).

34 James Hamilton to Abercorn, 27 January 1769, (D/623/A/38/117).

35 James Hamilton to Abercorn, 3 March 1769 (D/623/A/38/119).

36 Abercorn to N. Nisbitt, 20 March 1754 (D/623/A/14/111).

37 Abercorn to N. Nisbitt, 9 December 1758 (D/623/A/16/17).

38 James Hamilton to Abercorn, 19 March 1767 (D/623/A/37/63).

39 Abercorn to James Hamilton, 12 April 1767 (D/623/A/18/90).

40 James Hamilton to Abercorn, 28 December 1773 (D/623/A/40/124).

41 James Hamilton to Abercorn, 18 September 1761 (D/623/A/35/50).

42 Petition from tenants in the parishes of Donagheady and Leck[patrick] to Abercorn, 24 Dec 1787 (D/623/A/47/49).

43 James Hamilton to Abercorn, 7 January 1788 (D/623/A/47/51).

44 James Hamilton to Abercorn, 9 March 1788 (D/623/A/47/59).

45 James Hamilton to Abercorn, 20 April 1788 (D/623/A/47/62).

46 James Hamilton to Abercorn, 10 January 1785 (D/623/A/46/1).

47 W. H. Crawford, 'The case of John McNeelans of Shanoney, 1773' in *Ulster Folklife*, xxiii (1977), pp 92–96. The letters from James Hamilton to the earl are numbered under the Abercorn correspondence D/623/A/40/ and

individually identified as 11 June 1773 (/100); 18 July 1773 (/104); 13 August 1773 (/108); 20 August 1773 (110); and 3 October 1773 (/114). The sole letter from the earl to Jemmy Hamilton is numbered D/623/A/21/44 and dated 25 July 1773.

48 James Hamilton to Abercorn, 10 July 1772 (D/623/A/40/48).

49 James Hamilton to Abercorn, 25 July 1772 (D/623/A/40/50).

50 James Hamilton to Abercorn, 31 July 1772 (D/623/A/40/54).

51 James Hamilton to Abercorn, 27 September 1772 (D/623/A/40/62).

52 James Hamilton to Abercorn, 29 September 1772 (D/623/A/40/63).

53 James Hamilton to Abercorn, 2 October 1772 (D/623/A/40/64).

54 Abercorn to James Hamilton, 27 October 1772 (D/623/A/21/9).

55 James Hamilton to Abercorn, 31 October 1772, (D/623/A/40/68).

56 James Hamilton to Abercorn, 15 November 1772 (D/623/A/40/70).

57 James Hamilton to Abercorn, 4 December 1772 (D/623/A/40/71).

58 James Hamilton to Abercorn, 8 December 1772 (D/623/A/40/72).

59 James Hamilton to Abercorn, 11 April 1773 (D/623/A/40/89).

60 James Hamilton to Abercorn, 1 June 1773 (D/623/A/40/99).

61 Abercorn to James Hamilton, 20 June 1773 (D/623/A/21/40).

62 James Hamilton to Abercorn, 9 July 1780 (D/623/A/44/38).

IMPROVING THE ESTATE

1 See for example W. H. Crawford & B. Trainor (eds), *Aspects of Irish social history, 1750–1800* (Belfast, 1969), pp 10–17.

2 Abercorn to John Hamilton, 18 January 1774 (D/623/A/21/73).

3 N. Nisbitt to Abercorn, 3 May 1757 (D/623/A/32/72).

4 John Hamilton to Abercorn, no date [spring 1768?] (D/623/A/38/186).

5 William Brownlow to Abercorn, 8 August 1768 (D/623/A/38/82).

6 William Brownlow to Abercorn, 22 October 1768 (D/623/A/38/99).

7 John Hamilton to Abercorn, 27 November 1768 (D/623/A/38/109).

8 John Hamilton to Abercorn, 5 March 1773 (D/623/A/40/80 and /81).

9 Abercorn to James Hamilton, 20 March 1773 (D/623/A/21/25).

10 Abercorn to John Hamilton, 18 January 1774 (D/623/A/21/73).

11 Abercorn to James Hamilton, 7 April 1774 (D/623/A/21/86).

12 W. A. McCutcheon, *The canals of the north of Ireland* (Dawlish, 1965), p.87.

13 James Hamilton to marquess of Abercorn, 23 November 1790 (D/623/A/86/21).

14 J. Colhoun to Abercorn, 2 May 1746 (D/623/A/28/15).

15 9 Anne c.9 s.9.

16 W. Harris, *The antient and present state of the county of Down* (Dublin, 1744), p. 77.

17 Abercorn to J. Colhoun, 1 August 1750 (D/623/A/13/76).

18 Abercorn to N. Nisbitt, 29 November 1750 (D/623/A/13/83).

19 Abercorn to J. Colhoun, 29 January 1751 (D/623/A/13/86).

20 9 Anne c.9 s.9; 1 George II c.13 s.9; 33 George II c.8 s.9.

21 Abercorn to N. Nisbitt, 17 April 1752 (D/623/A/14/68).

22 James Hamilton to Abercorn, 18 March 1758 (D/623/A/33/15).

23 James Hamilton to Abercorn, 18 April 1758 (D/623/A/33/22).

24 James Hamilton to Abercorn, 21 November 1758 (D/623/A/33/57).

25 5 Geo.III, c.14.

26 James Hamilton to Abercorn, 31 October 1766 (D/623/A/37/46).

27 Abercorn to James Hamilton, 12 April 1767 (D/623/A/18/90).

28 James Hamilton to Abercorn, 11 April 1773 (D/623/A/40/89).

29 James Hamilton to Abercorn, 23 June 1769 (D/623/A/38/141).

30 James Hamilton to Abercorn, 5 January 1772 (D/623/A/40/3).

31 James Hamilton to Abercorn, 14 March 1784 (D/623/A/45/16).

32 J. Colhoun to Lord Paisley [who became earl of Abercorn in 1744], 21 August 1736 (D/623/A/5/10).

33 J. Colhoun to Abercorn, 15 November 1747 (D/623/A/28/59).

34 Abercorn to J. Colhoun, 29 January 1751, (D/623/A/13/86).

35 Michael Priestley to Abercorn, 15 June 1757 (D/623/A/32/82).

36 N. Nisbitt to Abercorn, 22 July 1757 (D/623/A/32/87).

37 James Hamilton to Abercorn, 9 June 1758 (D/623/A/33/31).

38 James Hamilton to Abercorn, 15 November 1772 (D/623/A/40/70).

39 James Hamilton to Abercorn, 8 December 1772 (D/623/A/40/72).

40 James Hamilton to Abercorn, 7 November 1784 (D/623/A/45/44).

41 James Hamilton to Abercorn, 9 January 1778 (D/623/A/43/82).

42 E. Gauldie, *The Scottish country miller, 1700–1900* (Edinburgh, 1981), pp 43–4.

43 James Hamilton to Abercorn, 28 November 1784 (D/623/A/45/46).

44 James Hamilton to Abercorn, 27 April 1759 (D/623/A/33/84).

45 Abercorn to John Sinclair, 7 October 1761 (D/623/A/17/34).

46 James Hamilton to Abercorn, 28 July 1758 (D/623/A/33/39).

47 William Sinclair to Abercorn, 29 May 1780 (D/623/A/44/35).

48 James Hamilton to Abercorn, 19 December 1780 (D/623/A/44/64).

49 James Hamilton to Abercorn, 22 December 1780 (D/623/A/44/66).

50 James Hamilton to Abercorn, 18 February 1781 (D/623/A/44/74).

51 James Hamilton to Abercorn, [September] 1781 (D/623/A/44/133); James Hamilton to Abercorn, 10 July 1785 (D/623/A/46/12).

52 *Journal of the House of Commons of Ireland, 1613–1791* (28 vols, Dublin 1753–91), viii, p. 37.

53 Galbraith Hamilton to Abercorn, 25 May 1779 (D/623/A/43/220).

54 James Hamilton to Abercorn, 1 October 1784 (D/623/A/45/42).

55 James Hamilton to Abercorn, 4 July 1784 (D/623/A/45/31).

56 James Hamilton to Abercorn, 26 October 1784 (D/623/A/45/43).

57 James Hamilton to Abercorn, 9 June 1785 (D/623/A/46/11).

58 James Hamilton to Abercorn, 17 November 1785 (D/623/A/46/18).

59 The letters written by N. Nisbitt to Abercorn between 15 April 1758 (D/623/A/33/20) and 31 October 1758 (D/623/A/33/54) contain regular comments on the progress of this project.

60 James Hamilton to Abercorn, 7 October 1768 (D/623/A/38/96).

61 James Hamilton to Abercorn, 18 May 1770 (D/623/A/39/38).

62 James Hamilton to Abercorn, 30 July 1776 (D/623/A/43/31).

63 Abercorn to James Hamilton. 26 August 1776 (D/623/A/22/81).

64 J. Colhoun to Abercorn, 22 December 1751 (D/623/A/30/129).

65 Abercorn to N. Nisbitt, 18 February 1752 (D/623/A/14/59).

66 John Hamilton to Abercorn, 18 November 1770 (D/623/A/39/82).

67 James Hamilton to Abercorn, 25 October 1771 (D/623/A/39/145).

68 A. W. Hutton (ed.), *Arthur Young's tour in Ireland 1776–1779*, (2 vols, London, 1892), i, pp 136, 138, 189; ii, pp 93–4.

69 James Hamilton to Abercorn, 29 January 1770 (D/623/A/39/9).

70 James Hamilton to Abercorn, 15 February 1788 (D/623/A/47/55) and 29 February 1788 (D/623/A/47/56).

71 James Hamilton to Abercorn, 17 November 1788 (D/623/A/47/76).

72 Address from the inhabitants of Strabane to Abercorn 1765 (D/623/A/36/165).

73 Abercorn to N. Nisbitt, 21 February 1751 (D/623/A/13/88).

74 A damaged document dated 17 October 1700 gives sufficient information to make this conclusion (D/623/A/2/1); R. M. Young (ed.), *Historical notices of old Belfast and its vicinity* (Belfast, 1896), p. 159.

75 Sixth earl of Abercorn to James Nisbitt, 15 January 1733 (D/623/A/5/10).

76 N. Nisbitt to Abercorn, 17 May 1753 (D/623/A/30/180).

77 N. Nisbitt to Abercorn, 8 December 1753 (D/623/A/30/204).

78 N. Nisbitt to Abercorn, 10 February 1753 (D/623/A/30/169).

79 James Hamilton to Abercorn, 5 July
   1759 (D/623/A/33/103).
80 J. Colhoun to Abercorn, 28 October
   1750 (D/623/A/30/40).
81 James Hamilton to Abercorn, 20
   October 1765 (D/623/A/36/152) and
   25 February 1770 (D/623/A/39/17).
82 James Hamilton to Abercorn, 24 April
   1770 (D/623/A/39/31).
83 James Hamilton to Abercorn, 10
   December 1775 (D/623/A/42/103).
84 Kelly, *Letters of Lord Chief Baron Edward
   Willes*, p.107.
85 T. Colby (ed.), *Ordnance Survey memoir
   of the county of Londonderry: parish of
   Templemore* (Dublin, 1837), p.268.
86 John Greer, *Report of the state of the linen
   markets in Ulster* (Dublin, 1784) with
   manuscript updating for 1803
   (PRONI, Foster Papers, D/562/6225).
87 James Hamilton to Abercorn, 9 March
   1764 (D/623/A/36/14).
88 John Hamilton to Abercorn, 3 May
   1765 (D/623/A/36/122).
89 John Hamilton to Abercorn, 5 June
   1765 (D/623/A/36/132).
90 John Hamilton to Abercorn, 12 January
   1766 (D/623/A/37/3).
91 James Hamilton to Abercorn, 14 July
   1771 (D/623/A/39/132).
92 John McEvoy, *Statistical survey of the
   county of Tyrone*, (Dublin, 1802), p. 188.
93 James Hamilton to Abercorn, 8
   November 1767 (D/623/A/37/106).
94 J. Colhoun to Abercorn, 26 March
   1751 (D/623/A/30/60).
95 James Hamilton to Abercorn, 7 June
   1768 (D/623/A/38/63).

96 J. Sinclair to Abercorn, 3 October
   1767 (D/623/A/37/99).
97 J. Sinclair to Abercorn 21 July 1769
   (D/623/A/38/145).
98 Abercorn to J. Sinclair, 13 August 1769
   (D/623/A/19/92).
99 J. Sinclair to Abercorn, 15 March 1770
   (D/623/A/39/21).
100 James Hamilton to Abercorn, 25
    February 1781 (D/623/A/44/75).
101 John Mc Farland to Abercorn, 27
    September 1790 (D/623/A/101/5), 24
    October 1790 (D/623/A/101/9), 6
    November 1790 (D/623/A/101/11);
    John McEvoy, Collon, county Louth
    to the marquess of Abercorn 15
    November 1790 (D/623/A/101/12).

CONCLUSION

1 Volume of 91 maps of the Abercorn
  estate in the manors of Donelong,
  Cloghogle, Strabane, and Derrygoon in
  the county of Tyrone, 1777, and
  Magavlin and Lismoghry in the county
  of Donegal, 1781, (D/623/D/1/16).
2 Note market juries (27 Geo.III c.46
  &28 Geo.III c.42), manor courts (25
  Geo.III c.44 & 27 Geo.III c.44), and
  parish vestries: fire engines (11&12
  Geo.III c.14), lighting, warding, and
  cleansing; institution of county
  infirmaries (5 Geo.III, c.20)
3 Malcomson, 'The politics of "natural
  right"', p. 78.

Maynooth Research Guides for Irish Local History

IN THIS SERIES

Maynooth Studies in Irish Local History

IN THIS SERIES

Maynooth Studies in Irish Local History (cont.)